THE UNDECIDED
COLLEGE STUDENT

THE UNDECIDED COLLEGE STUDENT.

AN ACADEMIC AND CAREER ADVISING CHALLENGE

By

VIRGINIA N. GORDON, Ph.D.

Coordinator of Academic Advising
University College
Ohio State University
Columbus, Ohio

CHARLES   C   THOMAS   •   PUBLISHER
Springfield • Illinois • U.S.A.

Published and Distributed Throughout the World by

CHARLES C THOMAS • PUBLISHER
2600 South First Street
Springfield, Illinois 62717

© *1984 by* CHARLES C THOMAS • PUBLISHER

ISBN 0-398-04989-0

Library of Congress Catalog Card Number: 83-24364

With THOMAS BOOKS *careful attention is given to all details of manufacturing and
design. It is the Publisher's desire to present books that are satisfactory as to their physical
qualities and artistic possibilities and appropriate for their particular use.* THOMAS
BOOKS *will be true to those laws of quality that assure a good name and good will.*

Printed in the United States of America
S-R-3

Library of Congress Cataloging in Publication Data

Gordon, Virginia N.
  The undecided college student.

  Bibliography: p.
  Includes index.
  1. Personnel service in higher education — United States.
2. Vocational guidance — United States.
3. College student orientation — United States. I. Title.
LB2343.G64 1984   378′.19425′0973   83-24364
ISBN 0-398-04989-0

To George, David, Cathy, Bob, and Jane

FOREWORD

The scattered attempts to help and study undecided students are analogous in many ways to the development of orphan drugs in medicine. Our knowledge of undecided students has proceeded slowly because there has been only sporadic interest in the necessary research and very little financial support for even that research. Most research has been the by-product of some "more important" research, and most of the programs and professional practices devised to provide assistance were stimulated by individual practitioners and researchers rather than by institutions.

The publication of this volume assembles for the first time the diverse speculation and theory, the research evidence, and the multiple organizational and professional practices for helping college students who have been characterized as "undecided, unwilling, or unable" to make appropriate educational and vocational decisions. Virginia Gordon has organized this diverse but substantial literature in a single volume. Academics, counselors, and researchers will no longer have to scrounge through a wide array of journals, books, and technical reports to obtain a comprehensive and systematic account of the research (old and new), the model programs for assisting students, and the diverse theory for understanding the undecided student.

This volume should stimulate the creation and evaluation of more informed and systematic vocational assistance. Most people will find the use of developmental speculation and theory to integrate and organize the services and techniques of academic advising to be congenial and plausible. Hopefully, this particular orientation will lead to more explicit evaluation as well as more explicit theory. And, whatever orientation a person adopts, the reader has a useful summary of all theoretical orientations.

JOHN L. HOLLAND

INTRODUCTION

Educationally and vocationally undecided students have been a focus for concern among college administrators, faculty, counselors, academic advisers, and parents for many years. A few view indecision as an unhealthy, worrisome condition, while others perceive it to be a perfectly natural, temporary state. It has been expedient on some campuses to force all new students to choose an academic major as they enter. Other colleges and universities have created categories or administrative units to identify initially and advise the students who honestly admit to being uncommitted to a specific direction. Some colleges even encourage students to make no commitment to a major their first year.

Undecided students themselves have mixed feelings. Some are scared, anxious, apologetic, and very negative about their situation. Others are open, flexible, and curious. They feel confident that the time spent exploring will be productive and in the end provide them with more a satisfying, stable decision.

Many students react to societal and parental pressures and make choices based on very little if any realistic information about their own abilities or the academic area they have selected. Still others deal with the "chicken and egg" question of not knowing which to select first—a career field or college major. Many students solve this dilemma by choosing an area in which the major and occupation are obviously and directly related.

Another large group of undecided students are those in the process of changing majors. On many campuses it is estimated that 50 to 70 percent of students change their major at least once. These students in transition are almost totally ignored programmatically on many campuses.

Undecided students are such a heterogeneous group and the administrative variations on campuses are so different that it is difficult to comprehend the enormity and complexity of trying to identify and advise them. Many problems are created because of the lack of understanding and respect for the diversity of this group. Few administrators gather data to create a profile of, or initiate needs assessments for, their undecided students. Few academic advisers and counselors have delved into the voluminous literature on the undecided student. Very often advisers work intuitively with undecided students and prescribe activities that may not be responsive to their needs. Many advisers are unaware of student development theory and how it explains some students' lack of readiness for making career and life decisions.

Why Help Undecided Students?

There are several issues involved in discussing the undecided student:

1. *There are significant numbers of them.* Current estimates range from 20 to 50 percent of the students entering college (Astin, 1977; Berger, 1967; Crites, 1969). These numbers reflect only those students who are honestly willing to admit their lack of readiness to state an academic or career direction. There are many more who would readily admit to being undecided if given the chance.

2. *Undecided students have been identified as attrition prone* (Astin, 1975; Beal & Noel, 1980). If offered no help, this group may drift and eventually drop out of college. Retention studies show that lack of a career goal is an important reason for not pursuing a college degree.

3. *Significant numbers of students change majors before they graduate.* These students are often undecided during this transition period. Studies have shown not only that this group is also attrition prone but that students delaying a change of major carry fewer credit hours and are lower achievers academically (Chase & Keene, 1981).

Throughout this book the term *undecided* is used as the descriptor for students unwilling, unable, or unready to make educational and/or vocational decisions, although many campuses use other terms to describe these students. Among these are *exploratory, open-major, deciding, undeclared, general education major,* and *special major*. The term *undecided* is used here because of its use in research and the easy identification with its meaning.

If one of the purposes of our colleges and universities is to help students set and implement educational and career goals, then we must be cooperatively engaged in that venture. Creating an environment that encourages and supports undecided students while they make important life decisions is central to that purpose.

REFERENCES

Astin, A. W. *Preventing Students from Dropping Out*. San Francisco: Jossey-Bass, 1975.

Astin, A. W. *Four Critical Years*. San Francisco: Jossey-Bass, 1977.

Beal, P. E., and Noel, L. *What Works in Student Retention*. Iowa City: American College Testing Program and the National Center for Higher Education Management Systems, 1980.

Berger, E. Vocational choices in college. *Personnel and Guidance Journal*, 1967, *45*, 888–894.

Chase, C., and Keene, J. Major declaration and academic motivation. *Journal of College Student Personnel*, 1981, *22*, 496–501.

Crites, J. O. *Vocational Psychology*. New York: McGraw-Hill, 1969.

CONTENTS

THE UNDECIDED
COLLEGE STUDENT

Chapter 1

WHO ARE UNDECIDED STUDENTS?

College students who are not committed to an educational or career direction have been studied since the 1920s. The research on undecided students, however, presents a "confusing picture" (Harman, 1973). Some investigators have found no differences in personality traits and ability measures between decided and undecided students. Others have found significant differences in personality factors and other variables. Reasons for this disparity may lie in the different ways in which writers define and understand *indecision*. It may also relate to the population they are examining (Gordon, 1982).

The research on indecision may be classified as studies on antecedents of indecision, characteristics that make undecided students different from decided ones, and treatments that have been initiated to facilitate becoming "decided."

Origins of Indecision

Antecedents of indecision have been examined in a variety of ways. Osipow (1973) suggests four reasons for "misdirected" career development as proposed by vocational theorists: (1) vocational choices that are inconsistent with the individual's self-information, (2) students' not keeping pace developmentally with their peers, (3) emotional instability, and (4) frozen behavior between two desirable choices. Osipow sees retarded rate of development as the reason that causes the most difficulty.

Holland (1973a) is very explicit about indecision in career choice. If two career choices are of equal strength or if the first is blocked and no second choice is present, indecision will result. An over- or underestimation of an individual's abilities for the vocational choice could also lead to conflict in vocational decision making.

3

Ginzberg et al. (1951) discuss deviant and variant choice patterns. The deviant pattern indicates general indecisiveness rather than a specific state of indecision. The variant pattern indicates delayed crystallization of vocational choice, which can be considered a normal process.

LoCascio (1964) uses the terms *impaired* and *delayed* to denote the same two patterns of vocational choice. Delayed development describes an individual who is unaware of, or not ready to learn, the developmental tasks associated with making a choice. Impaired development is similar to Ginzberg's deviant pattern in that the individual has not mastered the vocationally relevant tasks necessary to make a choice, and little learning occurs.

Tyler (1953) postulates a number of antecedents for vocational indecision. She suggests that opinions and attitudes of family and friends can act as deterring factors. For example, a parent's expectations may create a situation that prevents a student from deciding. A cluster of reasons for indecision may emanate from not accepting or not being satisfied with the role that the occupation represents, even though the skills and activities within the occupation are appealing. Sex-role stereotyping of occupations may be a factor, too. Tyler also discusses the multipotential individual who is interested and talented in many directions and finds it difficult, if not impossible, to narrow down the alternatives. Another cause of indecision, according to Tyler, might be not accepting realistic limitations or obstacles that stand in the way. After accepting the fact that a particular decision is impossible, the person may be more open to considering other options.

Tyler distinguishes between indecision and indecisiveness, the etiology of the two being totally different. Indecisiveness is a result of unsatisfactory habits or thinking that permeates the individual's total life. Until these personal problems or uncertainties can be resolved, a career or educational decision cannot be reached. Tyler also comments upon the place of immaturity in indecisiveness and how choices are a part of developmental sequences. A person will not be able to make later decisions if earlier ones are not resolved.

Zytowski (1965) submits that some indecision might be explained by avoidance behavior. Some individuals avoid committing themselves to a career direction because the idea of working repels them or they have a fear of career commitment.

Certain persons gain psychological satisfaction from leisure or nonwork involvements. Contrary to the middle-class value system, a vocation is not the main source of satisfaction for some individuals, especially those brought up in the lower social classes, where work only satisfies certain biological needs. Not choosing a vocation might signify an avoidance of the issue.

Appel, Haak, and Witzke (1970) identify the factors associated with indecision concerning an academic major or career choice. Their *Career Decision Readiness Inventory* samples dimensions of decision-making behavior. They propose six meaningful factors describing undecided students: (1) situation-specific choice anxiety, (2) data-seeking orientation, (3) concern with self-identity, (4) generalized indecision, (5) multiplicity of interests, and (6) humanitarian orientation. This study serves to point out that multiple causes of indecision exist and that undecided students constitute a heterogeneous group.

Vincent Harren (1966) explores the theoretical assumptions of Tiedeman and O'Hara's vocational decision-making model (1963). To study the antecedents of indecision, it is necessary to understand the "internal processes, functions and mechanisms inferred from an individual's vocational behavior" (p. 271). Tiedeman's and O'Hara's paradigm examines the concept of vocational decision making as a process that exhibits certain stages.

Harren has developed an instrument to measure Tiedeman's vocational stages (1966, in press). The studied areas of decision making are choice of academic major and choice of occupation. Harren finds students at the exploration, crystallization, choice, and clarification stages as Tiedeman has described them. Most students look upon choosing a major and an occupation as a single problem. Harren speculates that those who treat these two choices as separate problems are either at different stages in each choice or else do not see the two as related. Harren concludes that the stages proposed by Tiedeman and O'Hara do exist but cautions that the problem is more complex than this simple model suggests. An important implication is that students at different vocational decision-making stages (such as undecided) require different counseling and guidance approaches.

One of the factors associated with indecision by Appel, Haak, and Witzke is situation-specific anxiety. Much of the research on anxiety and occupational choice has focused on how an individual's anxious state deters or inhibits the decision-making process.

A concept proposed by Goodstein (1965) has received much consideration. Goodstein identifies two groups of undecided individuals. The first type is undecided for a number of reasons, such as vocational immaturity or lack of readiness for the developmental tasks necessary to form a decision. For this person, the inability to reach a decision provokes a feeling of anxiety. Societal or educational pressures to make a choice intensify his or her anxiety. This person simply needs occupational information or help in learning decision-making skills. According to Goodstein, such an individual is experiencing indecision, and a variety of experiences or information should provide the needed help. The anxiety associated with the choice process would consequently be alleviated.

The second type of undecided person described by Goodstein is the indecisive one. This individual finds the anxiety associated with the choice process debilitating and has difficulty reaching a decision about anything. Contrasted to the person who is undecided and anxious about this lack of decision, the indecisive individual finds the decision-making process and commitment itself anxiety arousing.

Goodstein describes anxiety associated with vocational choice as free-floating anxiety that is delimited in this specific area. Anxiety cues are difficult to identify in this process, and the individual is hard pressed to identify the exact circumstances of anxiety arousal. Nonadaptive behavior regarding the lack of vocational plans is often seen by counselors as stemming from a void of prior experience that could have provided the opportunity to learn responses. As Goodstein points out, however, before an indecisive individual can make a choice, factors contributing to existing personal-social conflicts must be dealt with.

Kimes and Troth (1974) investigate the relationship between career decisiveness and trait anxiety. They find that students who have a career in mind but are not moving toward a decision and those who have not made a career decision have a significantly higher mean trait anxiety score than those who have definitely decided. Students who are completely undecided have the highest mean trait anxiety score. As the level of anxiety proneness increases, the level of decidedness decreases. Kimes and Troth conclude that high anxiety-prone individuals may have more difficulty in making occupational choices than individuals who are less anxiety prone.

Hornak and Gillingham (1980) treat career indecision as self-defeating behavior. Students rationalize their lack of responsibility for not deciding by citing lack of concentration, labeling, blaming others, comparing and distorting feedback, and relying on external evidence or forces. Habitual use of these negative techniques, according to Hornak and Gillingham, reinforces indecisive behavior. A more positive approach is for the students to become involved in the decision-making process so that they may learn responsibility for their own behavior.

More recent approaches to explaining the origins of indecision deal with assessing the reasons that individuals provide for educational and occupational indecision (Hartman & Fuqua, 1982; Holland & Holland, 1977; Jones & Chenery, 1980). These diagnostic schemes view indecision as stemming from multiple factors such as lack of vocational identity, informational deficits, lack of motivation, external barriers, and career salience. Several instruments have emerged to help identify and measure the level of intensity of specific antecedents that students offer for their being undecided. These diagnostic instruments include the *Career Decision Scale* (Osipow et al., 1976) and *My Vocational Situation* (Holland, Daiger, and Power, 1977).

Characteristics of Undecided Students

Other research concerned with indecision describes the characteristics of the undecided student. A great many earlier investigations of indecision were parts of studies intended to research other problems (Crites, 1969). Achilles (1935), Kilzer (1935), Williamson (1937), Sisson (1941), and Kohn (1947) look at correlates of indecision such as scholastic standing, background information, and other influences while investigating topics other than indecision.

Nelson and Nelson (1940) find a relationship between social, moral, and religious attitudes and vocational choice. Students choosing certain occupations such as banking, dentistry, music, and government service prove more conservative than students who choose journalism, social work, law, and agriculture. Undecided students place near the middle of this distribution. Miller (1956) compares the choice of work values among students who are undecided and those who are tentatively or definitely decided. The "no-choice" group tends to emphasize security and prestige, while those who have formulated a choice place higher value on career satisfaction.

Risk-taking tendencies as they apply to decision making are examined by Ziller (1957). Groups of college sophomores who are decided and undecided on career choice show significant differences on the risk aspect of the choice process. The lower risk-takers are the undecided group.

These earlier studies concentrate on various correlates of decision rather than on undeciding persons or the levels of their indecision. In more recent years, researchers have viewed indecision as an important topic itself and have tried to identify characteristics common to indecision. One of the earliest studies is that undertaken by Holland and Nichols (1964). The purpose of their investigation is to validate an indecision scale, but in the process some of the personal characteristics of undecided individuals are identified. The subjects used in this research are National Merit finalists, who are asked to respond to activities in which they "frequently, occasionally, or never engaged." Items are identified that appear to describe a cluster of personal traits common to undecided students. Some of these include a socially oriented cluster, an artistic-creative cluster, and an aggressive cluster of activities. The researchers point out that, in the past, indecision was identified with confusion, illness, and the need for counseling. This study suggests that, for some people, indecision is an aspect of the rate of personal development and that intellectual curiosity and creativity are characteristics of students who cannot narrow their interests.

In a widely quoted study dealing with indecision in college freshmen, Ashby, Wall, and Osipow (1966) categorize their subjects into three types: decided, tentatively decided, and undecided. The study's objective is to compare personality traits and background characteristics among these three kinds of students. Variables included in the study are interest patterns, personality traits, self-ratings on Holland's personality types, academic abilities, high school information, and family background data such as parents' income and education.

The three groups demonstrate no differences on the personality, school, and family background variables; however, they are differentiated by academic ability and achievement. The decided and undecided students are academically superior to the tentatively decided ones.

Ashby, Wall, and Osipow conclude that the antecedents for being undecided and tentatively decided are important considerations in understanding a student entering college. The reservations that the tentatively decided students have about their choices are rooted in knowledge of their academic deficiencies. The undecided, on the other hand, are considered academically capable but need help with formulating a choice. Ashby, Wall, and Osipow find them more dependent than the other two groups. These results have ramifications for counseling approaches and treatments for different types of students.

Using a large national sample of over 12,000 college freshmen, Baird (1967) studies the characteristics of undecided students as they compare to those of students who have made a vocational choice. The students are tested with a wide variety of measures including the *Vocational Preference Inventory*, extracurricular achievements, competency scales, range of experiences, indecision, dogmatism, life goals, and aspirations. Undecided male students are found to be slightly less interested in science. Both undecided men and women are not "vocationally oriented." Other than these two factors, the overwhelming conclusion of the study is that no real differences exist between students who have decided on a vocation and students who have not.

Baird (1967) not only examines the personality differences between decided and undecided college freshmen but also investigates differences in academic aptitude and educational goals. The students' American College Test (ACT) scores and high school grade point averages are used, as well as statements concerning students' goals in attending college. No differences are indicated on the mean of the composite ACT score. However, the undecided students emphasize the college goal of developing their minds and intellectual abilities more often than that of choosing a vocational or professional goal. Thus, undecided students seem more intellectually and less vocationally oriented.

Contrary to former beliefs (Williamson, 1939), these studies point out that the undecided student is not necessarily more emotionally immature or less intellectually able. No differentiation appears in interest patterns or background variables between the decided and the undecided college freshman.

Holland and Holland (1977) submit that students who consider themselves undecided do not differ in any group of personal characteristics except in terms of their own sense of identity and vocational maturity. Holland and Holland suggest that researchers have spent their energies looking for specific variables that describe undecided students as a single type when instead they should be looking at broad patterns of variables that indicate multiple subtypes.

Most of the research cited above deals with students who are undecided before entering college or during their freshman year. Looking at another subgroup, Lunneborg (1975) compares undecided college graduates three months after graduation with those who have chosen a vocation. The undecided graduates seem to be students who do not do as well in college, are less satisfied with their college experience, and are not as motivated by vocational goals while in college. No differences emerge between the decided and undecided graduates as to when they choose a major or the amount of paid employment they experience prior to graduation. The undecided graduates are not motivated to seek out career-related activities for their future.

Another study involving graduating seniors is that completed by Elton and Rose (1970). Undecided students are identified as freshmen and followed up as they approach graduation. Three groups of graduating seniors are discussed: those who are undecided as freshmen, those whose senior choice changes from an earlier one, and those whose choice remains constant. No differences are found on personality or ability measures, and those who are undecided eventually make a choice consistent with their ability, according to the study.

Program Interventions

A third aspect of the research dealing with indecision is the development of career decision interventions that are designed to help a person decide. Vocational counseling services and programs have greatly expanded over the past decade. A variety of interventions is practiced in the elementary and secondary schools, colleges and universities, technical and community colleges, rehabilitation centers, and social agencies and is now offered by private consulting firms as well. The proliferation of these programs, methods, strategies, and resources is apparent from the number of program descriptions and research studies in the recent literature.

Holland (1973) categorizes vocational interventions as (1) vocational information or guidance systems, (2) special programs for special populations, (3) curricular materials, (4) career education, and (5) assorted assessment tools, such as tests, inventories, and information materials. Holland criticizes many current vocational planning services as not helping the people they are designed to reach. He claims they do not involve many people who need them, are too expensive, have little effect, and are often inefficient. He places some of the blame on the outdated practices of counselors who cling to one-on-one counseling. He also claims that many counselors now look upon the trait-factor approach as an outmoded model; in Holland's opinion, it is still one of the most useful and time-tested tools available in vocational counseling.

Miller and Benjamin (1975) outline strategies for life-career development programs in a different way. They view career development as a lifelong process that involves people of all ages and life-styles. They point out the need for services in a variety of learning settings and a new accountability in evaluating these services. Among the interventions they recommend for meeting these new and expanded needs are: (1) achievement motivation training, (2) self-assessment techniques, (3) career resource learning centers, (4) career development curriculum, (5) decision-making training, (6) media approaches, such as simulations, computerized programs, and audiovisual materials, and (7) value clarification techniques. Miller and Benjamin conclude that a systematic approach to program development can be the most effective method for implementing vocational interventions.

The expanded role in which counselors now find themselves in the career development area requires them to update or acquire new competencies. A study by the American Institute for Research (Mitchell, 1975) identifies the many skills that an individual needs to move through the various phases of career decision making. Any intervention effort must recognize the importance of teaching these skills (Kroll et al., 1970), which include: self-awareness and understanding of the world of work, interpersonal skills, employment skills, coping skills for the future, goal-setting skills, and decision-making skills. In order to help people acquire, maintain, and implement these skills, Mitchell lists career counseling, program planning, program implementation, consultation, community linkage, staff development, and evaluation competencies as crucial areas for improving counselor expertise. Mitchell recognizes that changes must be effected in counselor education, philosophy, goals, and course instruction before this needed training can be implemented. Crites (1981) presents a comprehensive model for career counseling that uses concepts and techniques from many major approaches. Crites summarizes these systems through their use of diagnosis, process, and outcomes. He offers a more comprehensive approach that would apply to all types of clients in a variety of situations.

A great surge of intervention descriptions has appeared in the literature since 1970. One fairly recent development at the college level has been the career-planning course. Since the tightening of the job market for college graduates has led many undergraduates to seek vocational counseling, the career course helps to meet this need. Examples of this approach have been provided by Bowlsbey Spivack, and Lisansky (1982), Comos and Day (1976), Figler (1975), Kravatsy and Magoo (1976), Velcich and Mitchell (1976), and Winefordner (1980). A few of these programs have gathered research data to evaluate systematically the effectiveness of these courses (Babcock and Kaufman, 1976; Barker, 1981; Graff, 1970; Smith and Evans, 1973; Stoddard, 1974). The course approach is popular with students since the academic credit provides incentives to complete the treatment.

A multiple-element career-planning course has been designed as an intervention for educationally and vocationally undecided university freshmen by Gordon, Carney, and Archibald (1974). They postulate that undecided freshmen receiving a highly structured career development experience become more decided and display greater educational-vocational information-seeking behaviors. The undecided students are compared to a group of Arts and Sciences freshmen who did not receive the treatment.

The class module uses self-assessment exercises, including a life-planning workshop, the *Self-Directed Search* (Holland, 1977), and educational and vocational information sessions. While the Arts and Sciences students are more decided and measure higher in vocational information-seeking behaviors on the pretest, the undecided students demonstrate significant movement toward the measured criterion on the posttest. The Arts and Sciences students show no change in level of decidedness or information-seeking behaviors on the posttest.

The group approach to career counseling has also been reported in greater frequency in recent years (Kuehn, 1975; Hazel, 1976; Velcich and Mitchell, 1976). The group format usually provides structured experiences and involves the students in specific tasks. These groups vary in duration and length of meeting time. As in the case of the career course, very few studies have been initiated on the effectiveness of such programs (Davidshofer, Thomas, and Preble, 1976).

Other methods of career-planning intervention reviewed in the literature are more innovative or meet special needs. Examples of these are a parent's workshop on vocational choice (Lea, 1976), computer-assisted vocational exploration programs (Harris, 1968; Pilato and Myers, 1975; Super, 1974), self-administered vocational counseling (Holland, 1973; McGowan, 1974), and decision-making models (Harren, 1966; Weissman and Krebs, 1976).

Vocational counseling interventions aimed specifically at the undecided student have been most thoroughly researched. One of the objectives of these interventions is to assist the undecided student to move closer to an educational or vocational decision. These treatments have incorporated a variety of methods and approaches. McGowan (1974) attempts to test the relationship of career indecision and indecisiveness with anxiety and vocational maturity. He finds that, while the self-administered treatment (*Self-Directed Search;* Holland, 1977) is effective in reducing indecision, no differential relationship seems evident between indecisiveness and anxiety and vocational maturity.

Mendonca and Seiss (1976) try various counseling procedures for reducing anxious vocational indecision. Anxiety-management training teaches subjects generalized skills of coping with anxiety. Desensitization techniques are used to negate anxiety reactions associated with decision making. Problem-solving training consists of understanding the decision-making process and learning appropriate responses to situations that require problem solving.

Mendonca and Seiss find that a combination of problem-solving and anxiety-management training is the most effective treatment. Students who develop a combination of anxiety-coping skills and decision-making skills exhibit more vocational exploratory behavior and more specific knowledge of their own career plans than students who receive only the problem-solving or anxiety-management procedures alone.

Using Blau et al.'s (1959) model for organizing decision-making skills in a conceptual framework, Jackson (1976) attempts to identify the specific skills needed in the decision-making process. She maintains that career maturity and IQ have a moderately high relationship to decision-making competencies. Jackson uses her process model in teaching a minicourse. Upon completion of the treatment, students say they are cognizant of more occupational choices, know how to obtain pertinent information, recognize and use values in reaching decisions, consider and rank alternatives, and realize that their first and second choices may not be the best ones for them. Females score higher than males in career maturity, decision-making skills, and educational and occupational aspiration after the treatment. Jackson concludes that the minicourse program based on Blau's conceptual framework increases self-understanding and occupational exploration behaviors.

Smith and Evans (1973) study the effects of two types of treatments on vocational development. The two treatment forms are: (1) a five-week guidance program that deals with decision making, vocational interests, values, behavioral traits, and social influences and their effects on choice status and (2) individual counseling. A control group is used to account for extraneous learning in everyday experiences that might occur over the five-week period. The five-week program has been found more effective in increasing vocational maturity scores on Harren's *Vocational Decision Making Checklist* (1972) than individual counseling; however, individual counseling is more effective than no treatment at all.

Winer (1975) investigates the effectiveness of deliberate vocational psychological intervention as compared to cognitive treatment. Two career-planning course formats are used to compare approaches. The affective component in the curriculum is viewed as an important factor in the career decision-making process. The students in the study are measured in career decision, career maturity, and moral judgment. Winer finds that students in the cognitive-plus-affective curriculum are more decided and show an increase in maturity as measured by Crites's *Career maturity inventory* (1978) or in general personal development as defined by Kohlberg's moral development stages (1969). The students exposed to the cognitive curriculum only do not measure any differences after the treatment. Winer concludes that effective decision making is facilitated by the cognitive-plus-affective curriculum, while general development is not. She recommends that further programmatic counseling interventions be studied, since they show promise as a career development intervention.

An important factor in measuring the effectiveness of career development interventions is the evaluation criteria that are used. Implicit in any effort to assist undecided students in making educational and vocational decisions is the assumption that the treatment will help them select goals that will lead to satisfaction with their choices. However, it is difficult to test methodologically the outcomes of these decisions (Gonyea, 1962; Super, 1974).

Hewer (1966) points out that realism or appropriateness of vocational choice has been used as a criterion for judging the effectiveness of counseling treatments. Hewer cites dissatisfaction with this criterion as a valid measure of effective vocational counseling over a period of time. She maintains that vocational choice is in a constant state of change and, therefore, difficult to measure in this way.

To test the long-range effects of a vocational counseling intervention, Hewer has performed a follow-up study on individuals who received vocational counseling eight years earlier. She measures realism of choice by the extent to which individuals remain in their chosen occupation. The frequency of fulfillment of goals set eight years earlier is surprising: By the criterion of employment in the same occupational level, nearly two-thirds of the individuals in this study are doing what they planned to do. Hewer concludes that realism of vocational choice is a suitable criterion for judging the effectiveness of vocational counseling.

The most important outcome of individual career counseling or program interventions is to assist the student in making a satisfying and realistic educational and/or occupational decision: Developmental approaches, however emphasize the choice *process*, not the choice *content* (Crites, 1981). The acquisition of decision-making skills is seen as a desirable outcome in many developmental interventions. Recent research indicates that career decision skills mediate the reasons for indecision and affect the level and type of decisions a person makes at a given time (Ware, 1980; Ware & Pogge, 1980). Perhaps the most useful intervention might be to help undecided students become aware of their unique and highly personal approach to the decision-making process itself (Gordon, 1984).

The diagnostic tools that have been developed in recent years show great promise in helping counselors design interventions that can be tailored specifically to an individual undecided student's needs. By understanding the reasons for indecision, advisers can provide a more personalized approach. The advantage of being able to pinpoint causes of indecision is that modular or group approaches may be created and implemented for many populations and settings.

Summary

Vocational theorists have approached the educational and career decision-making process from many perspectives. While some researchers have emphasized personality characteristics, others have concentrated on economic and sociological factors. A developmental approach recognizes life stages and tasks and behaviors accomplished at each of these stages. A lifelong career decision-making approach recognizes that an individual's personality in tandem with the environmental pressures he or she faces at a given time influences not only the choice itself but also the mechanics of the decision.

Career indecision is viewed from three perspectives. Research on the origins of indecision provides data on possible psychological antecedents. A second aspect of career indecision deals with the characteristics that describe the undecided student. The research here is contradictory. Some studies conclude that the undecided student is no different than the decided one, while others demonstrate differences in personality traits and demographic variables. Newer approaches are concentrating on the multiple subgroups within the undecided population and the manner in which decision-making skills mediate the influences that have import on the process at a given time.

Career decision interventions may be discussed in the context of program types, timing, and populations. Programs designed to assist undecided students have grown rapidly over the past decade. The career development course as a method for intervention has gained in popularity. New diagnostic tools show great promise for helping counselors identify the reasons students are undecided and create specific interventions to meet the needs of individual students.

Overall, the research on undecided students, while voluminous, has yielded little in characterizing this heterogeneous group in specific terms. Perhaps this in itself is important to understand in developing interventions and programs to serve them.

REFERENCES

Achilles, P. Vocational motives in college career decisions among undergraduates. *Occupations*, 1935, *13*, 624–628.

Appel, V., Haak, R., and Witzke, D. Factors associated with indecision about collegiate major and career choice. *Proceedings, American Psychological Association*, 1970, *5*, 667–668.

Ashby, J., Wall, H., and Osipow, S. Vocational uncertainty and indecision in college freshmen. *Personnel and Guidance Journal*, 1966, *44*, 1037–1041.

Babcock, R., and Kaufman, M. Effectiveness of a career course. *Vocational Guidance Quarterly*, 1976, *25*, 261–267.

Baird, L. *The Undecided Student — How Different Is He?* ACT Research Report No. 2. Iowa City: American College Testing Program, 1967.

Barker, S. An evaluation of the effectiveness of a college career guidance course. *Journal of College Student Personnel*, 1981, *22*, 354–358.

Berger, E. Vocational choices in college. *Personnel and Guidance Journal*, 1967, *45*, 888–894.

Blau, P. M., Gustad, J. W., Jessor, R., Parnes, H. S., and Wilcock, R. C. Occupational choice: A conceptual framework. *Industrial Labor Relations Review*, 1959, *9*, 531–543.

Bowlsbey, J. H., Spivack, J., and Lisansky, R. S. *Take Hold of your Future*. Iowa City: American College Testing Program, 1982.

Comos, E., and Day, R. College students explore careers. *Vocational Guidance Quarterly*, 1976, *25*, 76–79.

Crites, J. *Vocational Psychology*. New York: McGraw-Hill, 1969.

_____. *Theory and Research Handbook for the Career Maturity Inventory*. Monterey: CTB/McGraw-Hill, 1978.

_____. *Career Counseling: Models, Methods and Materials*. New York: McGraw-Hill, 1981.

Davidshofer, C., Thomas, L., and Preble, M. Career development groups: A program description. *Journal of College Student Personnel*, 1976, *17*, 413–419.

Elton, C., and Rose, H. Male occupational constancy and change: Its prediction according to Holland's theory. *Journal of Counseling Psychology*, 1970, *17*, 6.

_____. A longitudinal study of the vocationally undecided male student. *Journal of Vocational Behavior*, 1971, *1*, 85.

Figler, H. *Path*. Cranston, Rhode Island: Carroll Press, 1975.

Ginzberg, E., Ginsburg, S. W., Axelrod, S., and Herman, I. L. *Occupational Choice*. New York: Columbia University Press, 1951.

Goodstein, L. Behavior theoretical views of counseling. In B. Steffre (Ed.), *Theories of Counseling*. New York: McGraw-Hill, 1965, pp. 140–192.

Gonyea, G. Appropriateness of vocational choice as a criterion of counseling outcome. *Journal of Counseling Psychology*, 1962, *9*, 213–219.

Gordon, V. Are undecided students changing? *Vocational Guidance Quarterly*, 1982, *30*, 265–271.

———. Educational planning and decision making. In R. Winston, T. Miller, & S. Ender (Eds.), *Academic Advising and Student Development.* San Francisco: Jossey-Bass, 1984.

Gordon, V., Carney, C., and Archibald, R. *A Multiple Element Career Planning Class Module for Educationally and Vocationally Undecided University Freshmen.* Paper presented at the American Psychological Association Convention, New Orleans, 1974.

Graff, R. Vocational-educational counseling practices: Survey of university counseling centers. *Journal of Counseling Psychology,* 1974, *21,* 569–580.

Harman, R. Students who lack vocational identity. *Vocational Guidance Quarterly,* 1973, *21,* 169–173.

Harren, V. The vocational decision-making process among college males. *Journal of Counseling Psychology,* 1966, *13,* 271–277.

———. *The Vocational Decision Making Checklist.* Unpublished manuscript, Southern Methodist University, 1972.

———. A model of career decision making for college students. *Journal of Vocational Behavior,* 1979, *14,* 119–133.

———. *Assessment of Career Decision-Making Manual* Los Angeles: Western Psychological Services, in press.

Harris, J. The computerization of vocational information. *Vocational Guidance Quarterly,* 1968, *17,* 12–20.

Hartman, B., and Fuqua, D. The construct validity of the career decision scale adopted for graduate students. *Vocational Guidance Quarterly,* 1982, *31,* 69–77.

Hazel, E. Group counseling for occupational choice. *Personnel and Guidance Journal,* 1976, *54,* 437–438.

Hewer, V. Evaluation of a criterion: Realism of vocational choice. *Journal of Counseling Psychology,* 1966, *13,* 289–294.

Holland, J., and Nichols, R. The development and validation of an indecision scale: The natural history of a problem in basic research. *Journal of Counseling Psychology,* 1964, *11,* 27–34.

Holland, J. L. *Making Vocational Choices: A Theory of Careers.* Englewood Cliffs, N.J.: Prentice-Hall, 1973a.

———. Vocational guidance for everyone. *Educational Researcher,* January, 1973b, *3,* 9–15.

———. *Self-Directed Search.* Palo Alto, California: Consulting Psychologists Press, 1977.

Holland, J. L., and Holland, J. E. Vocational indecision: More evidence and speculation. *Journal of Counseling Psychology,* 1977, *24,* 404–414.

Holland, J. L., Daiger, D., and Power, P. *My Vocational Situation.* Palo Alto, California: Consulting Psychologists Press, 1977.

Hornak, J., and Gillingham, B. Career indecision: A self-defeating behavior. *Personnel and Guidance Journal,* 1980, *59,* 252–253.

Jackson, D. *Process Verification of a Career Counseling Program.* Paper presented at the annual meeting of the American Education Research Association, San Francisco, 1976.

Jones, L., and Chenery, M. F. Multiple subtypes among vocationally undecided college students. A model and assessment instrument. *Journal of Counseling Psychology*, 1980, *27*, 469–477.

Kilzer, L. Vocational choices of high school seniors. *Educational Administration and Supervisors*, 1935, *21*, 576–581.

Kimes, H., and Troth, W. Relationship of trait anxiety to career decisiveness. *Journal of Counseling Psychology*, 1974, *21*, 277–280.

Kohlberg, L. Stage and sequence: The cognitive-developmental approach to socialization. In D. A. Goslin (Ed.), *Handbook of Socialization Theory and Research*. Chicago: Rand McNally, 1969.

Kohn, N. Trends and development of the vocational and other interests of veterans at washington university. *Educational and Psychological Measurement*, 1947, *7*, 631–637.

Kravatsy, S., and Magoo, T. Differential effects of three vocational counseling treatments. *Journal of Counseling Psychology*, 1976, *23*, 112–118.

Kroll, A., Dinklage, L., Lee, J., Morley, E., and Wilson, E. *Career Development: Growth and Crises*. New York: Wiley, 1970.

Kuehn, J. Group counseling of undecided college students. *Vocational Guidance Quarterly*, 1975, *24*, 232–235.

Lea, H. A personalized parent's workshop on vocational choice. *Vocational Guidance Quarterly*, 1976, *25*, 373–375.

LoCassio, R. Delayed and impaired vocational development: A neglected aspect of vocational development theory. *Personnel and Guidance Journal*, 1964, *42*, 885–887.

Lunneborg, P. Interest differentiation in high school and vocational indecision in college. *Journal of Vocational Behavior*, 1975, *7*, 299–303.

McGowan, A. Vocational maturity and anxiety among vocationally undecided and indecisive students: The effectiveness of the *Self-Directed Search*. *Dissertation Abstracts International*, 1974, *35*, 2691–2692.

Mendonca, J., and Seiss, T. Counseling for indecisiveness, problem-solving, and anxiety-management training. *Journal of Counseling Psychology*, 1976, *23*, 339–347.

Miller, C. H. Occupational choice and values. *Personnel and Guidance Journal*, 1956, *35*, 244–246.

Miller, J., and Benjamin, L. New career development strategies: Methods and resources. *Personnel and Guidance Journal*, 1975, *53*, 694–699.

Mitchell, A. Emerging career guidance competencies. *Personnel and Guidance Journal*, 1975, *53*, 700–703.

Nelson, E., and Nelson, N. Student attitudes and vocational choices. *Journal of Abnormal and Social Psychology*, 1940, *35*, 279–282.

Osipow, S. *Theories of Career Development* (2nd ed.). Englewood Cliffs, N.J.: Prentice-Hall, 1973.

Osipow, S., Carney, C., Winer, J., Yanico, B., and Koschier, M. *Career Decision Scale* (3rd revision). Columbus, Ohio: Marathon Consulting and Press, 1976.

Pilato, G., and Myers, R. The effects of computer-mediated vocational guidance procedures on the appropriateness of vocational preferences. *Journal of Vocational Behavior*, 1975, *6*, 61–72.

Sisson, E. Vocational choices of students from cities, towns, and farms. *School and Society*, 1941, *54*, 94–96.

Smith, R., and Evans, J. Comparison of experimental group guidance and individual counseling as facilitators of vocational development. *Journal of Counseling Psychology*, 1973, *20*, 202–208.

Stoddard, K. *A Career and Life-planning Seminar.* Unpublished manuscript, University of Utah, 1974.

Super, D. E. *Measuring Vocational Maturity for Counseling and Evaluation.* National Vocational Guidance Association. Washington, D.C.: American Personnel and Guidance Association, 1974.

Tiedeman, D., and O'Hara, R. *Career Development: Choice and Adjustment.* New York: College Entrance Examination Board, 1963.

Tyler, L. *The Works of the Counselor.* New York: Appleton-Century-Crofts, 1953.

Velcich, J., and Mitchell, M. Mini-term: Exploring career choices. *Vocational Guidance Quarterly*, 1976, *24*, 371–373.

Ware, M. E. Antecedents of educational/career preferences and choices. *Journal of Vocational Behavior*, 1980, *16*, 312–319.

Ware, M. E., and Pogge, D. L. Concomitants of certainty in career related choices. *Vocational Guidance Quarterly*, 1980, *28*, 322–327.

Weissman, S., and Krebs, D. A decision-making model for career exploration. *Personnel and Guidance Journal*, 1976, *54*, 517–520.

Williamson, E. G. Scholastic motivation and the choice of a vocation. *School and Society*, 1937, *46*, 353–357.

_____. *How to Counsel Students.* New York: McGraw-Hill, 1939.

Winefordner, D. *Career Planning and Decision Making.* Bloomington, Illinois: McKnight, 1980.

Winer, J. *Cognitive and Cognitive-plus-affective Curricula and the Facilitation of Career and General Development.* Unpublished doctoral dissertation, Ohio State University, 1975.

Ziller, R. Vocational choice and utility for risk. *Journal of Counseling Psychology*, 1957, *4*, 61–64.

Zytowski, D. G. Avoidance behavior in vocational motivation. *Personnel and Guidance Journal*, 1965, *43*, 746–750.

Chapter 2

ADMINISTRATIVE MODELS
AND SCOPE OF SERVICES

There are many administrative vehicles, program approaches, and advising services needed to help undecided students make realistic, satisfying, and stable educational and vocational decisions. The following questionnaire, "Assessing Your Advising Program for Undecided Students," will help assess the comprehensiveness and scope of the services provided the undecided students on a particular campus campus. The item(s) that describe the program should be checked. Scoring instructions are at the end of the questionnaire.

ASSESSING YOUR ADVISING PROGRAM FOR UNDECIDED STUDENTS
1. What administrative provisions do you make for undecided students? (Select one.)
_____ a. A separate enrollment unit specifically created for them
_____ b. A unit designated for undecided students within a college (Arts and Sciences, Agriculture, etc.)
_____ c. The same way decided students enroll—directly in a college or department
_____ d. We do not administratively recognize students as undecided.
2. Do you have special orientation session(s) for your entering undecided students? (Select one.)
_____ a. Yes
_____ b. No
3. As part of your orientation program, what activities do you provide for undecided students? (Check each that applies.)
_____ a. Special group scheduling sessions
_____ b. Parent information sessions
_____ c. Introduction to the special services offered undecided students.
_____ d. Individual advising
_____ e. We do not offer special sessions for undecided students.
4. Do you have a written policy or set of objectives for advising undecided students? (Select one.)

_____ a. Yes
_____ b. No

5. What delivery system do you use to advise undecided students? (Check each that applies.)
   _____ a. Randomly assigned faculty advisers
   _____ b. Faculty advisers who volunteer to work with undecided students
   _____ c. Designated advisers in an advisement center
   _____ d. Advisers in a unit specifically created for undecided students
   _____ e. We do not officially recognize students as undecided.

6. Is one person assigned either part-time or full-time to coordinate the advising services for your undecided students? (Select one.)
   _____ a. Yes
   _____ b. No

7. How do you provide academic information to your undecided students? (Check each that applies.)
   _____ a. Regularly scheduled group sessions with faculty in many areas
   _____ b. As part of a freshman orientation or career-planning course
   _____ c. Referral to individual faculty in many areas
   _____ d. Work individually with adviser
   _____ e. We don't have any organized program for exploring academic options.

8. How do you provide career exploration and planning for your undecided students? (Check each that applies.)
   _____ a. Special workshops to help them explore career fields
   _____ b. Career-planning course for credit
   _____ c. Access to the same career services as regular students
   _____ d. Program involving contact with workers in a variety of occupations in the community
   _____ e. Career library
   _____ f. Computerized career information system
   _____ g. Field experience courses for exploring occupational fields in person
   _____ h. No special programs

9. Do you conduct a specific training program for advisers of your undecided students? (Select one.)
   _____ a. Yes
   _____ b. No

10. What topics do you typically cover in your training sessions? (Check each that applies.)
   _____ a. Student development concepts
   _____ b. Campus referral sources
   _____ c. General academic major information including scheduling priorities and information about each major

_____ d. Career development concepts
_____ e. Humanistic advising skills
_____ f. Career information and employment outlook
_____ g. Decision-making models

11. How frequent are your training sessions for advisers of undecided students? (Select one.)
_____ a. Once a year
_____ b. Twice a year
_____ c. Once a month
_____ d. More than once a month

12. What type of support materials do you provide the advisers of your undecided students? (Check each that applies.)
_____ a. Special advising manual for undecided students
_____ b. Academic-planning sheets for all majors
_____ c. Campus resource referral lists
_____ d. Community resource lists
_____ e. Computerized student information system
_____ f. No special materials

13. What materials do you routinely provide advisers for undecided students? (Check each that applies.)
_____ a. ACT/CEEB Student Profile Reports
_____ b. High school transcripts
_____ c. College transcript/grade reports
_____ d. Self-assessment test results (interests, abilities, personality, etc.)

14. What is your estimate of the frequency of contact between advisers and undecided students on your campus? (Select one.)
_____ a. Once a year
_____ b. Twice a year
_____ c. Five to seven times a year
_____ d. More than eight times a year

15. When do your advisers have contact with undecided students? (Check each that applies.)
_____ a. Registration
_____ b. When they drop or add a course
_____ c. When they declare a major
_____ d. When they withdraw
_____ e. At least two other times per term for discussing progress
_____ f. Regularly, their first term, in a freshman orientation course

16. How do you monitor the academic and career exploration progress of an individual undecided student? (Check each that applies.)
_____ a. Through regularly scheduled conferences with adviser
_____ b. By checking their courses when they schedule
_____ c. Through declaration of major cards

17. Do you formally evaluate your program for undecided students? (Select one.)

　　_____ a. Yes
　　_____ b. No

18. If yes, how do you evaluate? (Check each that applies.)

　　_____ a. Advisee evaluation
　　_____ b. Research studies on advisee's progress as stated in your objectives
　　_____ c. Adviser evaluation
　　_____ d. Administrative review of your program

SCORING

Question	Points	Question	Points	Question	Points
1. a.	3	8. a.	1	13. a.	1
b.	1	b.	2	b.	1
c.	0	c.	0	c.	1
d.	0	d.	1	d.	1
		e.	1		
2. a.	3	f.	3	14. a.	0
b.	0	g.	2	b.	0
		h.	0	c.	3
3. a.	1			d.	5
b.	1	9. a.	3		
c.	1	b.	0	15. a.	1
d.	1			b.	0
e.	0	10. a.	1	c.	1
		b.	1	d.	1
4. a.	5	c.	1	e.	3
b.	0	d.	1	f.	5
		e.	1		
5. a.	0	f.	1	16. a.	5
b.	1	g.	1	b.	0
c.	3			c.	0
d.	3	11. a.	0		
e.	0	b.	0	17. a.	3
		c.	1	b.	0
6. a.	5	d.	3		
b.	0			18. a.	1
		12. a.	1	b.	3
7. a.	1	b.	1	c.	1
b.	3	c.	1	d.	1
c.	1	d.	1		
d.	1	e.	1		
e.	0	f.	0		

Sum the total number of points you scored.

If you scored between 80 and 90 points you probably need this book only to refine the excellent practices you already employ. Lower scores indicate this book may provide ideas and suggestions for creating an environment in which successful exploration and decision-making can be practiced.

90–80   Outstanding Program
70–79   Good
60–69   Fair
0–59   Poor

Delivery Models

The American College Testing Program conducted a national survey (Crockett, Silberhorn & Kaufmann, 1981) to determine the various administrative vehicles for meeting the advising needs of undeclared majors. Forty-five percent of the 420 institutions responding report that a general or special advising center is used to advise students who have not determined their majors. The majority of institutions, however, report no special advising services for this population. Other units or offices responsible for the advisement of these students include the registrar, admissions office, colleges or departments, special service centers, academic affairs offices, and student affairs office. Several of these delivery models are described below, with some advantages and disadvantages given for each.

General Advising Center

Advisement centers have been established in recent years to provide advising continuity and stability for all students (Baxter, 1971; Carstensen & Silberhorn, 1979; Spencer, Peterson & Kramer, 1982). These centers are usually staffed by full-time professional advisers, but faculty, peer, and paraprofessional advisers often augment advising center staffs (Crockett, 1982; Grites, 1979).

In addition to general advising, advising centers often offer services to special groups of students such as the undecided population. The advantages of this system for these students are many. Information is easily accessible and current. The continuity of contact with well-trained professional advisers who are knowledgeable about many academic areas is especially advantageous to undecided students. Advising centers are often able to provide the integration of academic and career information that is vital to an exploring student.

Advising centers provide an easily recognized, central location for services for all students. Some students hesitate to identify themselves as undecided; an advising center provides the type of anonymity that these students prefer. There are many levels of decision among freshmen; the advising center can offer a wide range of services while providing the specialized information that many students require. This system is especially helpful to the student who changes majors and needs special help during this transition period.

Disadvantages of an advising center for undecided students include the lack of faculty contact that students need (Miller & Brickman, 1982; Tinto, 1982). This can be overcome, however, through careful programming and referral. Another disadvantage is the direct cost of maintaining such a center (Crockett, 1982). When student retention is an issue, however, advisement centers have proved to be an extremely effective method for providing comprehensive services to all types of students (Pino, 1975; Shelton, 1972). The advantages of a centralized system thus far outweigh the disadvantages.

Faculty Advising

The oldest and most commonly used vehicle for providing academic advising services is still the faculty advising system. Faculty members are considered the most knowledgeable and appropriate individuals for providing academic information, scheduling help, and long-range program planning. Many recent studies, however, have focused on the problems inherent in a faculty advising system (Mahoney, Borgard & Hornbuckle, 1978; Moore, 1972; Stickle, 1982). Since many faculty advisers are subject matter oriented, this creates a distinct disadvantage to the undecided student who may wish to explore several unrelated academic areas.

While many faculty advisers are student centered and provide a very personalized approach to program and course selection, they often lack the background knowledge and skills needed to advise undecided students. Advising these students requires a great deal of concentrated time and effort. Unfortunately, faculty are infrequently rewarded for the time spent in advising. This creates a certain amount of pressure on conscientious faculty who are already involved in teaching, research, and committee assignments.

When faculty are used to advise undecided students, they must be selected on the basis of their willingness to work with this special group, must be aware of the time and effort involved, and must be willing to attend frequent training and in-service programs to develop their expertise in advising this group. Faculty advisers to undecided students need to become generalists in academic information, become knowledgeable about student development theory and practice, and understand career development as well as career and academic relationships. They need to maintain up-to-date and accurate information about the academic programs at their institution. These faculty need to be rewarded for the additional time and energy this system requires (for example, a decreased course load or monetary rewards).

The advantage of a faculty advising system is the opportunity for student-faculty contact and a climate for establishing a relationship that is an important part of the college experience. When faculty advising is carefully integrated into other delivery systems such as an advising center, the best of all possible programs can be realized.

Advising Centers for Undecided Students

Twenty-one percent of the institutions in the American College Testing Program's national survey indicate they have created a special center specifically for advising undeclared majors. Undecided students are identified through the admissions process or during orientation. These students are then assigned to the special center (Bonar & Mahler, 1976; Menning & Whittmayer, 1979).

Advising centers specifically designed to meet the needs of undecided students provide certain advantages. Early identification of students means that they may become involved in special programs and services immediately. A special center provides:

1. An identifiable location, so that exploratory students know

where services are available and can become familiar with the programs that are offered on their behalf
2. Specially trained professional advisers who are sensitive to the needs of this population
3. An organized approach to exploration, which can be initiated by adviser and student immediately
4. Continuity of contact with an adviser who knows the individual student's unique interests, abilities, needs, and values
5. Special program elements, which may be designed to offer a comprehensive service
6. Career exploration, which may be provided through special individual and group sessions or through career-planning courses for credit
7. A career library service, which can help students access current and accurate occupational and job market information. Computerized career information systems may be available as well
8. A means for initiating needs assessments as well as monitoring individual students' progress
9. An evaluation of services, which can provide information about the program's effect on student satisfaction and retention

Many of the above functions may also be provided by a general advising center. A general center that assigns advisers exclusively to the undecided population is frequently used for providing services for these students. The advantages of the special center, however, are that all efforts are concentrated on the undecided group and that specialists can be developed to work with a smaller population. Advisers in a special center are usually not from specific disciplines and therefore can advise from a student-centered perspective rather than being concerned about loyalty to a certain discipline. Full-time professional advisers are more apt to be trained in career as well as academic advising.

One disadvantage of a special center is that a few students do not wish to be identified as undecided and so do not use the services even though they need them. This can be overcome by creating a climate that encourages all students to explore during their freshman year and providing an atmosphere that supports students who are initially decided but who need to change majors later.

Further, a special center, like the general advising center, requires a direct cost that many small institutions, in particular, find difficult to justify for a small number of students. A combination of delivery systems including a special center for undecided students may be cost-effective, however, when the retention of students is considered.

Residence Hall Centers

Another vehicle for delivering coordinated services to undecided students is a residence hall program created especially for students who wish more concentrated help with academic and career planning (Abel, 1981). An advantage of such an approach is that entering freshmen can identify themselves immediately and participate on a voluntary basis. Small groups within the dorm may be formed early, and help with adjustment concerns as well as academic and career planning may be provided in a very personalized environment.

A freshmen orientation or career-planning course for credit can be taught in the residence hall. Classes can be held on the premises, and many career-related activities can be incorporated into the residence hall programming. A career resource library may be established in the center, so that students have easy access to many printed materials and other resources.

A residence hall center for undecided students can provide an ongoing, coordinated program effort that can meet the developmental needs of students during the freshman year. Upperclassmen who need a structured approach to career exploration could also be included as a separate component of the overall program.

A disadvantage of this delivery system is that many students who need this type of help do not wish to be identified in this way. It obviously eliminates the many commuter students who need this type of intensive advising service, as well.

University Colleges or Divisions

Some larger institutions have developed advising systems through a special college of enrollment, such as a "university college" or "university division" (Burns & Kishler, 1972, Gordon, Shreffler & Weaver, 1978). Not only are most entering freshmen provided advising services especially designed for their needs, but undecided students may be easily identified and served. Students wishing to commit themselves tentatively to a general academic area such as business, engineering, education, or the health professions may do so while taking general education requirements. Students may confirm their choice or change major with few bureaucratic limitations. A university college system offers all entering freshmen, whether decided or undecided, the same opportunity and time to identify, study, and confirm a major decision in a supportive, carefully supervised environment (Menning & Whittmayer, 1979).

A university college system may provide the best delivery method for academic and career advising for undecided students, since many of the resources for exploring can be provided within one physical location. Referral for academic information may be made within the college, since most academic areas are represented by advisers trained to advise in specific major fields. Freshman orientation courses can also be taught within the context of a university college (Minnick, 1983), and career counseling and career information resources may also be provided. Many university colleges are also responsible for the orientation of new students, so the undecided group can be easily identified and assigned as they enter advising services designed especially for them.

The university college system recognizes that many freshmen need the time to explore and confirm educational and vocational decisions. Advisers within a university college system are trained to work with freshmen students and become specialists in advising this population. Undecided students are able to explore in a well-coordinated program while not feeling separated from their classmates.

Other Delivery Systems

Other areas that advise undecided students, identified in the American College Testing Program's national survey, include individual colleges or departments and academic and student affairs offices. Undecided students who must choose a specific degree college or academic department while exploring may find limited help in gathering information about a wide variety of unrelated majors. Advisers in colleges or departments are rarely generalists and can only refer a student with interests outside their expertise to other departments or faculty. This creates a fragmented approach to the search process and may discourage the student from looking beyond the confines of the enrollment unit. While this system is better than none, it severely limits and complicates the exploration process.

Academic and student affairs offices are also less desirable, since the expertise of academic affairs advisers is generally limited to academic information. Student affairs professionals will be able to provide the personalized, student developmental perspective that is essential to the advising process, but they may not have access to the complex academic information that undecided students need.

The delivery system selected by an institution to advise undecided students will depend on the importance it attaches to these special students; its philosophy regarding the right of, and the need for, individuals to explore; and the resources, both human and financial, that it is willing to allocate to this function. Special or general advising centers that target programs for the undecided are increasingly recognized as effective vehicles for providing the type and extent of academic and career advising that undecided students require. Once the delivery method is established, there are certain administrative considerations to take into account. Setting program objectives, selecting, training, and evaluating staff, creating and refining program elements, and evaluating the effectiveness of the overall effort are a few of the areas to consider. The need for one individual to coordinate this overall program quickly becomes apparent.

Administrative Considerations

Regardless of the delivery system that is used, there are certain administrative factors that need to be considered for effective operation of an academic advising program.

1. *A program philosophy and a set of objectives based on this philosophy need to be established.* Such a philosophical statement for a program might include the following:

a. Not declaring a major or career field when entering college is acceptable and for some students encouraged.

  b. Exploring students may spend time and will receive organized help in assessing their personal strengths and limitations as they relate to major and occupational choice.

  c. Exploring students may spend time and receive help in researching information about a variety of academic majors and career areas.

  d. Exploring students will make an academic decision within a time frame that is developmentally theirs.

Objectives must be developed to put this philosophy into action. Possible objectives include:

By the beginning of their sophomore year, entering exploratory students will—

  a. understand the career development process as it relates to different stages of their lives, especially the college years.

  b. have gained insights and knowledge about their own decision-making styles and strategies.

  c. have learned and practiced information-seeking behaviors.

  d. have considerable information about majors gathered and have discussed these majors with faculty or college counselors in at least three areas.

  e. have chosen a major or narrowed their choice to several realistic alternatives.

  f. express satisfaction with the advising help they have received during the exploration process.

Another set of objectives would need to be developed for each group of students, such as those who change majors or are undecided upperclassmen. It is difficult to evaluate the effectiveness of an advising program without a written policy or objectives statement. While these objectives may change periodically, they serve as a framework within which the various services and activities may be developed.

  2. *The staff needed to initiate and maintain a program for undecided students may be composed of full-time professional advisers, faculty, graduate students, peer advisers, or a combination of these.* One professional staff member must be designated to coordinate the program.

No matter how large or small the institution or the effort, a program without this coordination cannot function effectively or be accountable.

In a national survey of 226 campuses conducted by George Mason University (Carretta, Looney & Sutera, 1983) under the auspices of the National Academic Advising Association, the titles reported for professionals responsible for coordinating services for undecided students include director/coordinator of advising (47%), college dean, department chairperson, and director of student counseling. Most of these coordinators report to a vice-president or dean of academic affairs.

Administrators or coordinators of an advising program for undecided students may be trained in academic advising philosophy and functions or career development and counseling, have knowledge and experience in testing and administration, and be able to bring together in one concerted effort all areas on campus engaged in working with this population. On smaller campuses this may be a part-time position, while in a setting with larger numbers of undecided students, a full-time professional administrator may be required.

The staff working with undecided students should be professionally trained advisers or counselors. Undecided students not only need generalists in academic information but also need advisers with a solid foundation in student and career development concepts, as well as knowledge for securing and interpreting career and job market information. In addition to excellent communication skills, counseling techniques are often required in certain situations. If faculty members are working with undecided students, they need to be trained in these areas as well. The number and type of staff vary greatly with the institution's resources and the number of students being served.

3. *Creating, developing, and refining program components are continuous processes.* On some campuses, certain programs and services are already in existence. Some campuses offer academic information sessions, decision-making workshops, or career-planning courses to all students, for example, and undecided students may become involved in these or in special adaptations designed for them. Other program components need to be initiated where

these services do not already exist. Testing resources, small-group advising sessions, or special sections of a freshmen orientation course might be created just for undecided students. These components need to be carefully coordinated to present a comprehensive, unified program.

A team approach is necessary to advising undecided students since their needs cut across many academic departments and student services. Every academic department on campus needs to become involved as a resource for undecided students, through printed information about their majors and requirements, and as a referral source, as students require in-depth information about their alternatives. Advisers, faculty, admissions and orientation personnel, counseling and testing resources, administrators, and career librarians all interact with undecided students throughout the academic year.

Community resources are also important in the overall advising of undecided students. For example, field experience sites as well as exposure to workers in a variety of careers may be used as components of a career exploration program. Health and social agencies, counseling resources, and other educational institutions are other community resources that may be integrated into student services.

Coordination of these services is critical if they are to function as a unified effort. Duplication or overlap of services is not as likely with careful supervision of the overall program.

4. *Program and staff evaluation must be carried out on a regular basis.* Evaluation of each program component as well as periodic assessment of the total program provides information on which to decide to retain certain successful elements and to make future changes. Soliciting student and staff evaluations of the program provides different perspectives in measuring the effectiveness of the overall effort. Periodic evaluation of advisers' effectiveness also needs to be initiated. (Chapter 5 describes evaluation techniques in more detail.)

Once the delivery method is established and objectives, staff, and program components are identified, services need to be organized and implemented. The scope of services begins with the first admissions contact and ends with the implementation of a decision by the student. Follow-up services may be necessary for certain students as well.

Scope of Services

There are many contact points for identifying and intercepting undecided students. Since some students enter college undecided and others become undecided after an initial choice is rejected or thwarted, services need to be available at many junctures.

Pre-entry Considerations

The first contact many students have with an institution is through the literature published to attract and provide information to prospective students. A clearly defined statement of the institution's philosophy toward exploration in catalogs and other printed materials alerts students and parents to the option of not declaring a major initially. Actively recruiting undecided students may be a positive activity, also. Admission contacts encouraging exploration must be backed by services and programs that will help students accomplish this task, however. A description of the counseling services available to all students is usually incorporated into an admissions brochure. Special descriptions of programs for the exploring student may also be included. The extent to which and emphasis with which this information is provided may affect the number and type of students willing to enter a specific institution undecided (Gordon, 1982).

Parents are often an integral part of the admissions process. Some students feel a great deal of pressure to choose a major from parental and other sources. Educating parents to the role of self- and academic information in the decision-making process and describing the type of help students can receive during the exploration period helps to alleviate some of their concerns. Parents are often fearful of a student losing time or "wasting courses" if he or she does not decide upon a major immediately upon entering college. While this may be true in isolated cases, parents need to be assured that the time taken for exploration may lead to a more stable and satisfying result. Admissions contacts can be an important time to help parents understand the tentativeness of many initial decisions and the possibility for future changes.

Most recruiting efforts include high school visitations and bringing prospective students on campus for informational programs. Many informal preadmissions contacts are made as well. The institution's philosophy on being uncertain about major or career decisions and the advising and counseling services offered can be described during these activities. Knowing these services are available may positively influence a student's decision to attend an institution.

Orientation

New student orientation is another critical point at which parents and students make major decisions. It is estimated that over 20 percent of all students change majors between admissions and the start of classes (Gelso & Sims, 1968). Orientation can be an important time to assure students that not being sure of their major at this point is a natural state and that specific help is available over a period of time to help them make choices in an orderly way.

Some institutions offer preorientation workshops at which academic and career information is provided. Some workshops incorporate self-assessment activities as well. While this offers a very superficial exposure to majors and requirements, it helps to take the mystery out of what appears to be a complicated and confusing body of information.

Special orientation sessions are especially enlightening to parents of undecided students since many are concerned about their child's lack of commitment and view undecidedness from a perspective rooted in another generation. Once they realize that their student will not wander aimlessly but will participate in an organized program for exploring, these fears are usually alleviated.

Academic Advising

Advising services involve many offices on campus. A unified effort is essential if the advice students receive is to be consistent, current, and appropriate. Areas that may become involved in advising the undecided student include academic departmental offices, individual faculty, counseling centers, residence halls, offices of records, and libraries. Each office or resource contributes to the advising function. Departmental offices and faculty can act as sources of information about programs, majors, and courses. Student affairs involvement may provide special programs in residence halls, while counseling centers may offer individual counseling and testing as well as workshops on such topics as self-assessment and decision making. Accurate and up-to-date student record keeping is also an important academic advising service. This includes not only the central record keeping for each student but also the records kept by each advisor for the individual students they advise. On large campuses, the variety and scope of services are undoubtedly broader, and the services more decentralized, than on smaller campuses.

Career Advising

The scope of career advising services extends from psychological counseling of students with career concerns to the teaching of a career-planning course for academic credit. Several areas on campus may be involved in providing a comprehensive career-counseling and information service to students. These include the counseling service, the career-planning and placement center on campus, and the library system, which provides specialized career information in an easily accessible format.

Integrating academic and career information is an important part of the advisement process. This requires the cooperation of both academic and career advising services. The George Mason survey (Carretta, Looney & Sutera, 1983) mentioned earlier asked how this task is accomplished on various campuses and tried to identify the obstacles that prevent this integration on a service level. Many campuses provide programs that are jointly sponsored by academic and career services. These include academic and career information, "career days," career decision-making courses, and major-planning workbooks.

Some obstacles to cooperation mentioned by the respondents to the George Mason survey include limited staff, turf-related problems such as reporting to different supervisors, no overall coordination, and a lack of priority on the part of the institution. Communication between academic and career services personnel is cited as important to the effective coordination of academic and career services. Personal contacts, written information, professional compatibility, proximity of offices, and administrative support are noted as conducive to encouraging this communication and coordination process.

Placement Services

The placement function on many campuses is combined with career-planning services. Undecided students benefit from current information about the job opportunities implicit with certain majors. Placement offices can provide current information that reflects the placement of recent graduates. Most placement offices encourage freshmen to become familiar with their services. Placement directors are an excellent resource for undecided students since they can offer not only occupational information but also information about employers' requirements and preferences. They often provide seminars in job-hunting skills that can be helpful to students searching for summer jobs. Work experiences can provide students with firsthand knowledge about the career areas they are considering.

Summary

There are many possible administrative models for delivering advising and counseling services to undecided students. Some campuses use existing faculty advising systems while others create a special administrative unit for this purpose. A combination of systems is also used, such as faculty advisers and full-time professional counselors in an advising center. Regardless of the delivery system, certain administrative considerations must be recognized as important to an effective program.

Program objectives must be established before advising services can be identified and created. A person designated to coordinate and monitor a program for undecided students is critical if a unified approach is to be achieved. Staff associated with the program must be carefully selected and trained. A team approach is required since so many offices and departments on campus are involved in working with undecided students.

The scope of services involved in working with undecided students begins with the first recruitment and admissions contact, includes the orientation of new students, and incorporates academic and career advising and placement services. Since the undecided students comprise a heterogeneous population and since their needs are so diverse, an efficient administrative system, the identification and implementation of a wide range of services, and the coordination and collaboration of many campus offices are essential if an effective program is to be initiated and maintained.

REFERENCES

Abel, J. Residence hall coordinators: Academic advising for undecided students. *NACADA Journal*, 1981, *1*, 44–46.

Baxter, R. P. A study of the emergencies and functioning of academic advising centers within academic units of major universities. *Dissertation Abstracts International*, 1971, *32*, 731A.

Bonar, J., and Mahler, C. A center for undecided college students. *Personnel and Guidance Journal*, 1976, *54*, 481–484.

Burns, K. N., and Kishler, T. C. *Centralized Academic Advising at Michigan State University*. East Lansing: Michigan State University, 1972.

Carretta, P., Looney, S., and Sutera, J. *Integrating Academic and Career Advising*. Fairfax, Virginia: George Mason University, 1983.

Carstensen, D., and Silberhorn, C. *A National Survey of Academic Advising*. Iowa City: American College Testing Program, 1979.

Crockett, D. S. Academic advising delivery systems. In R. Winston, S. Enter, and T. Miller (Eds.), *Developmental Approaches to Academic Advising*. San Francisco: Jossey-Bass, 1982.

Crockett, D. S., Silberhorn, C., and Kaufman, J. (Eds.) *Campus Practices for Students with Undeclared Majors*. Iowa City: American College Testing Program, 1981.

Gelso, C. J., and Sims, D. Faculty advising: The problem of assigning students on the basis of intended major. *Journal of College Student Personnel*, 1968, *9*, 334–336.

Gordon, V. N. Are undecided students changing? *Vocational Guidance Quarterly*, 1982, *30*, 265–271.

Gordon, V. N., Shreffler, N. L., and Weaver, W. J. *A Comprehensive Program of Academic Advising and Career Development for University Freshmen*. Paper presented at the annual convention of the American Personnel and Guidance Association, Washington, D.C., March 1978. (ERIC Document Reproduction Service No. 162216)

Grites, T. J., *Academic Advising: Getting Us Through the Eighties*. Washington: American Association for Higher Education Research Report, No. 7, 1979.

Mahoney, J., Borgard, J., and Hornbuckle, P. The relationship of faculty experience and advisee loads to perceptions of academic advising. *Journal of College Student Personnel*, 1978, *19*, 28–32.

Menning, A. J., and Whittmayer, C. Administrative and program provisions for undecided students. *Vocational Guidance Quarterly*, 1979, *28*, 175–181.

Miller, T., and Brickman, S. Faculty and staff mentoring: A model for improving student retention and service. *NASPA Journal*, 1982, *19*, 23–26.

Minnick, T. *University Survey: A Guidebook for New Students.* Columbus, Ohio: Ohio State University, 1983.

Moore, K. M. Faculty advising: Panacea or placebo? *Journal of College Student Personnel*, 1972, *23*, 262–265.

Pino, J. A, The organization, structure, functions, and student perceptions of the effectiveness of undergraduate academic advising centers. *Dissertation Abstracts International*, 1975, *35*, 4205A–4206A.

Shelton, J. *A Comparison of Faculty Academic Advising and Academic Advising by Professional Counselors: Final Report.* Shawnee Mission, Kansas: Johnson County Community College, 1972. (ERIC Document Reproduction Service No. 162216)

Spencer, R., Peterson, E., and Kramer, G. Utilizing advising centers to facilitate and revitalize academic advising. *NACADA Journal*, 1982, *2*, 13–23.

Stickle, F. Faculty and student perceptions of faculty advising effectiveness. *Journal of College Student Personnel*, 1982, *23*, 262–265.

Tinto, V. Limits of theory and practice in student attrition. *Journal of Higher Education*, 1982, *53*, 687–700.

Chapter 3

TYPES OF UNDECIDED STUDENTS

As determined in Chapter 1, undecided students comprise a diverse population. Each student may be considered unique, with special background, personal characteristics, and needs. This means that advising services must be as comprehensive and flexible as possible. One of the first steps in designing interventions is to obtain a profile of the students for whom services are being offered. Advisers on each campus must decide what characteristics are important to identify about their undecided students. This information is useful not only for immediate planning but also for comparing data and determining trends over an extended period of time.

Important information to collect includes the number and type of new freshmen who are openly committed to exploration as well as of other groups such as undecided upperclassmen and those in the process of changing majors. This chapter identifies multiple subgroups that can be found within the undecided population and describes some of their advising needs.

Entering Freshmen

Perhaps the largest and most obvious group is the traditional-aged freshmen who enter college unable, unready, or unwilling to commit themselves to a specific academic direction. This group can be easily identified through admissions information, SAT or ACT profile data, or surveys given during the orientation of new students. It is useful to determine their levels of indecision, reasons for enrolling college, and reasons for being undecided in order to develop advising services to help them. This information may be obtained through questionnaires or by using established instruments such as the *Career Decision Scale* (Osipow et al., 1976) and *My Vocational Situation* (Holland, Daiger & Power, 1977). Figure 1 provides an example of a brief orientation survey used for this purpose.

Once a student has openly admitted a willingness to explore, specific interventions may be offered, for example, individual advising, freshman seminar or career exploration courses, workshops, and academic information sessions. Chapter 5 provides detailed descriptions of these program components.

Although freshmen comprise one of the largest subgroups, they are often the easiest to approach. The first step in advising individual freshmen involves determining specific areas of need. These needs may be classified as informational deficits, developmental skill deficits, or personal or social concerns (Carney, 1975).

Informational Deficits.

Undecided students may lack information in three general areas: (1) They may need to assess their own personal characteristics, such as values and goals, interests, abilities, energy levels, and needs. (2) They may lack information about the academic areas that are available for study on a given campus. Although students are provided catalogs and other printed materials concerning majors, general requirements, scheduling, and other academically related tasks, they often need help interpreting or integrating this information. (3) A third informational deficit may be lack of knowledge about occupational areas. Understanding the daily tasks and being able to identify the rewards in a certain occupation are only two types of occupational information needed to make a choice.

Developmental Skill Deficits

Although some undecided students have sufficient information upon which to base a decision, they lack appropriate decision-making skills and are therefore unable to formulate a choice. Former decision-making experiences may have proved counterproductive. For example, an impulsive style may have been used when more reflection and thought were needed. Implementing educational and vocational choices is a developmental task with which many students need advising help. Taking responsibility for a decision once it is made is an important part of the process as well.

FRESHMAN ORIENTATION SURVEY

1. Male _____   Female _____

2. Age: 17–19 _____   23–25 _____
        20–22 _____   Over 25 _____

3. Married _____   Not married _____

4. In which third of your high school class were you?
   Highest third _____   Lowest third _____
   Middle third _____   Not sure _____

5. First-quarter freshman _____   Transfer _____

6. I will be living
   _____ in a residence hall
   _____ at home with parents or relatives
   _____ in own apartment or home

7. Why are you attending the university (*Check one.*)
   a. _____ To prepare for an occupation
   b. _____ To become an education person
   c. _____ Because my parents expect it
   d. _____ Because of the social opportunities
   e. _____ Because my friends are
   f. _____ To find myself
   g. _____ Other (please specify.) _____

8. How undecided are you about a major? (*Check one.*)
   a. _____ I am completely decided on an academic major.
   b. _____ I have an idea of what I wish to major in but am not ready to commit myself.
   c. _____ I have several ideas but cannot decide on one.
   d. _____ I am completely undecided about an academic major.

9. How undecided are you about an occupation? (*Check one.*)
   a. _____ I am completely decided about an occupation.
   b. _____ I have an idea about an occupation I wish to work in but am not ready to commit myself.
   c. _____ I have several ideas but cannot decide on one.
   d. _____ I am completely undecided about an occupation.

10. What kind of help would benefit you most in deciding on a major or occupation (*Check one.*)
    a. _____ Information sessions with faculty about various majors
    b. _____ Information sessions with workers in various careers
    c. _____ Career-planning classes to help me explore various options
    d. _____ Tests to help me find out what I'm interested in
    e. _____ Information sessions on employment opportunities
    f. _____ Talking with a career counselor
    g. _____ Actual field experience in a career area
    h. _____ Other (Please specify.) _____

FRESHMAN ORIENTATION SURVEY (*continued*)

11. For what career would you like specific information? (*Do not check more than three.*)

a. _____ Business		i. _____ Government
b. _____ Health Professions		j. _____ Law
c. _____ Social Service		k. _____ Law Enforcement and Criminology
d. _____ Education		l. _____ Agriculture
e. _____ Science		m. _____ Engineering
f. _____ Math		n. _____ Environmental/National Resources
g. _____ Computer Science		o. _____ Writing
h. _____ Art		p. _____ Other (Please specify.) _____

Personal-Social Concerns

Some students may be experiencing self-conflict in several ways: (1) They may have a values-goal conflict. They may want a job that provides a great deal of money, but their interests are in areas in which salaries are not large, such as teaching and social work. (2) They may have an interest-ability conflict. Their interests may be in areas for which they have marginal ability, or their strengths may be in areas for which they have no interest. They may have a great deal of aptitude for mathematics, for example, but have no interest in the occupational or academic areas related to this subject. (3) They may have an interest-energy level conflict. Some students may not have the energy level required to obtain their goal. An individual may want to become a physician, for example, but his or her energy level to perform in such a demanding profession may be in question. (4) Some students may have a conflict with significant other people whom they admire or want to please. They may not be able to separate their own needs and wishes from the "shoulds" and "oughts" of others.

One or several of these deficits could be the cause of a student's indecision. Raising awareness and identifying specific areas in which deficits exist is an important component of individual or group advising. Sometimes a student's personal or social concerns indicate a need for referral to a professional counselor for in-depth help. This is especially true of the student whom Goodstein (1965) identifies as *indecisive*. While the student experiencing indecision tends to have deficits in the informational and developmental skills areas, the indecisive student may need counseling for personal-social concerns or developmental problems.

While most advising is done with individual students, group advising can also be offered. The freshman orientation or seminar course is especially effective with entering students. The course approach to self-assessment and major exploration and planning can be provided in a structured setting during students' first weeks on campus. Too often undecided freshmen are not provided this type of supportive advisement immediately as they enter college.

Creating an open, supportive climate that encourages entering freshmen to explore alleviates some of the anxiety and pressure they feel. A developmental advising approach offers the opportunity and provides the services this group of students needs to make reasoned, well–thought-out educational and vocational decisions (Gordon, 1981). Chapter 4 focuses on this type of advising.

Major-Changers

Another important group of students beginning to receive long overdue attention is the students who enter college ostensibly decided about a major but change their minds during the college years (Foote, 1980; Kojaku, 1971; Slaney, 1980; Titley & Titley, 1980). Although it is estimated that these students comprise up to 75 percent of the college population, little has been written about who they are or how to advise or counsel them during this important period of transition.

Many students find that their ideas about an academic major or career field change as they progress through college. Students need to understand that initial decisions may be tentative and that changing their minds is not only acceptable but often desirable behavior. As Kojaku (1971) points out, this change could be logical and predictable.

It is often assumed that students who declare a major need little career assistance. Goodson (1981) finds, however, that decided students express the same need for help as undeclared students. In his survey of over 2,000 students, Goodson discovers that declared majors express the need for occupational information, help in assessing their own personal strengths and limitations, and help with the decision-making process. Vocational developmental theorists view this phenomenon as normal behavior (Ginzberg, 1972;

Super et al., 1963; Tiedeman & O'Hara, 1963). Many college students are in the midst of maturational and identity struggles; choosing an academic major from a myriad of choices is a developmental task for which they are not prepared.

Titley, Titley, and Wolf (1976) asked major-changers to specify the occupations they can enter with their new major as well as their old one. Overall, they are more specific about occupations relating to their new major than those relating to the former one, which, again, is consistent with vocational developmental theory (Super et al., 1963). Seniors, however, have a more difficult time specifying occupations than freshmen do, which is interpreted as an example of developmental continuity and discontinuity in the choice of career among college students (Tiedeman & O'Hara, 1963). Seniors are more knowledgeable about a variety of options, however, and become less dualistic in their approach to the process.

Chase and Keene (1981) study the differences in academic motivation between students who declare a major by the fifth semester of enrollment and those who do not. They find that students who postpone a declaration of major achieve lower grades and take fewer credit hours. Chase and Keene conclude that the lack of clear academic goals is associated with lower levels of academic achievement. Selecting a stable and realistic major is an important variable in the satisfaction, success, and retention of college students (Abel, 1966; Beal & Noel, 1980; Cope & Hannah, 1975).

Other studies (Hofman & Grande, 1979; Titley & Titley, 1980) point out that many entering freshmen express or experience uncertainty in selecting an academic major and/or career direction. Many of these students, however, succumb to parental and societal pressures and declare a major upon entering college. Since many of these decisions are based on little concrete information, it is inevitable that many of their ideas broaden and change during their college years.

The following descriptions are an attempt to speculate about some of the characteristics of these mind-changers. This is intended as a way of thinking about them theoretically. More research is needed to determine who they really are and what specific factors cause them to change their minds. Although it is dangerous to type students, the following descriptions are drawn from contacts with hundreds of students from diverse backgrounds. Academic advisers and career counselors may recognize some of the characteristics described in the following types of mind-changers.

Types of Major-Changers

THE DRIFTERS. Some students sense very early that their initial choice of college major is wrong but are reluctant to seek help to explore other possibilities. Some are working students with little time or energy to spend on exploration. Some do not feel pressures to seek out alternatives, while others simply do not know how. Some drifters procrastinate in other areas of life and put off making an alternative major choice until the system forces them to do so.

Adviser Interaction: Academic advisers need to be more sensitive to the drifters' existence. If allowed to wander too long, they become frustrated and remain without goals. Since they have no sense of direction, they are more apt to drop out of college.

The drifters need information about other majors and a great deal of help in organizing an orderly search. They may need to learn basic decision-making skills. Some drifters graduate and become occupational drifters, but if they learn in college how to clarify values, make decisions, and set goals, they have learned skills necessary to life itself.

THE CLOSET CHANGERS. Some students change their major in their head but tell no one, least of all their academic adviser. Students enroll in their new major for several terms but seek no help in scheduling or other important advising tasks.

Some closet changers are afraid to admit a major change because it is against the wishes of a significant other person. Others are unsure of their ability to handle the academic requirements and disguise their new intentions until they can prove (or disprove) themselves. A strange selection of courses may be a clue to advisers that a certain student is a closet changer.

Adviser Interaction: Closet changers often make choices internally without seeking help from external sources such as friends, academic advisers, or career counselors. Although they have decided on an alternative major in their heads, they do not publically commit themselves for many months. When closet changers are suspected, they need to be encouraged to confirm their new choice, to discuss scheduling with an adviser in their new area, and to take the appropriate action to change officially.

THE EXTERNALS. The externals change majors frequently. They consistently solicit advice from anyone who will offer it: They may hear about a new major from a roommate, a friend of their family, or a student in one of their classes. They appear totally unorganized about their search and express the fear that they may miss a major that they should consider.

Adviser Interaction: Sometimes the externals need to be confronted with their nonproductive approach to choosing a major and helped to organize a plan for exploration. They may need to be taught rational decision-making techniques. They should be encouraged to choose a major within a reasonable but definite length of time. Once they make a commitment, they need to acknowledge responsibility for their decision.

THE UP-TIGHTERS. Sometimes the major that students declare initially becomes unattainable or unrealistic. Their goals may be thwarted by rejection from a selective admissions area, or their abilities may not match their interests. This may be the only major they have ever considered, and they may feel depressed when they finally realize the futility of their situation. The up-tighters may resist examining alternatives at first, since it is difficult for them to accept reality.

Adviser Interaction: The up-tighters need a great deal of support and patience. Very often the emotional charge associated with changing majors needs to be acknowledged and dealt with before any other help is offered. The up-tighters may be helped to analyze what attracted them to their original choice and to find the same values or tasks in alternative majors or occupations. A positive, structured approach to exploring alternatives with a great deal of encouragement and support is often the best way to help them.

THE EXPERTS. The experts know everything. They rarely request help of any type. Even though their choice of major may be totally unrealistic in view of their abilities or other factors, they continue to act as though they were in complete control of the situation. They may try to enroll in higher level courses for which they have no background. Like the up-tighters, the experts are students who *need* to change their major since their initial choice is not attainable, but they refuse to accept this—at least on the surface.

Adviser Interaction: Working with the experts takes tact and sensitivity. Helping a student confront unrealistic aspirations is a difficult task. A nonjudgmental, encouraging attitude may help students realize that a change must be made and that there are alternatives that are just as viable and satisfying. Sometimes only a systems rule or regulation will force an expert to take action.

THE SYSTEMATICS. Systematics are students who acknowledge that their original major is wrong for them and take advantage of the academic and career advising services on campus. They realize the need for a coordinated approach for exploring alternative majors and go about it in an organized way. They gather information about possible alternatives, taking into consideration their own strengths and limitations. They discuss these alternatives with knowledgeable persons such as faculty or career advisors, but in the end the decision is theirs. They approach a decision with the right mixture of rational and intuitive thinking. They know the appropriate action to take once their decision is confirmed.

Adviser Interaction: Systematics are the kind of mind-changer that advisers enjoy working with since they are mature enough to take charge of the search for alternatives and accept responsibility for the decision once it is made. The ultimate goal of any adviser should be to help all mind-changers become systematics.

Helping Students in Transition

How can advisers help students who are in the process of changing their college major? There are several considerations that are important in advising or counseling this important group.

TIMING OF HELP. To students in transition, timing of help is critical. Advising help may be offered too early for some (who are not ready to acknowledge that their choice is unrealistic or unattainable) or too late for others (who drop out). Students who feel pressured to make a change in a hurry do not spend the quality of time necessary to examine alternatives. Other students, who have been permitted to drift too long, become depressed or discouraged because of their lack of a goal. Each student's timing is different. Help must be promptly available when students decide they are ready.

ADVISER ACCESSIBILITY. Adviser accessibility is related to timing but is important in itself. Students in the process of changing majors need to know where to go for help as soon as they decide to change. The human resources and services on campus to help these students must be easily identified and available when the student needs them.

INTENSITY OF NEED. Students are often emotionally involved in the idea of changing majors. They may feel they are letting someone down, or perhaps a lifelong dream is being shattered. The intensity of this emotional reaction needs to be acknowledged as natural, and help provided to deal with it. Otherwise, emotional barriers may impede the progress of a student in transition.

ADVISER ATTITUDES. Advisers working with students in transition need to possess positive attitudes about the change process. Advisers who view changing majors as a natural developmental phenomenon convey feelings of acceptance and support. Different advisers send very different messages (sometimes negative) in this regard. They usually do not possess the expertise necessary or else do not wish to deal with the problem. Help for these students is very random and unorganized across many campuses.

ADVISERS' EXPERTISE. Not all advisers have the knowledge and skill to work with major-changers. Students need an adviser who is a generalist in academic information, so that a wide variety of alternatives may be explored. Some students need a career adviser since their exploration may need to include an evaluation of their own personal strengths, interests, values, needs, etc.

Other specific ways for helping students in transition are:

1. *Help students rethink their goals.* If the goals associated with students' original major are no longer viable, they need to reorder their priorities and establish new goals. Clarifying values is an important part of this process.
2. *Help them generate new alternatives.* Advisers and career counselors can help students identify many majors that might satisfy their interests and abilities. Some majors may satisfy the same intrinsic values as the original major, but students

may need help in discovering these. If the student wants a totally new direction, alternatives need to be identified systematically and referrals made to faculty and other resources.

3. *Help them see how the credits they have already earned (if any) fit into other academic programs.* Students are often concerned about losing time or not graduating with their class. Since many general requirements may be used with many majors, students need to know how to adapt their credits to alternative programs.

4. *Help them understand the occupational implications of alternative majors.* Many students today are job oriented. They may have chosen their first major because of its direct connection to a specific occupation. This concern should be dealt with openly and realistically. Students are often unaware of the relationships between academic majors and career fields.

5. *Help them devise a plan of action.* This takes a great deal of help from many sources. In addition to academic information and faculty referral, students may need to talk to placement offices or workers in the community. They need help in identifying the specific action steps necessary to reach their new goals.

Some colleges and universities need to examine their admissions procedures for requiring students to make choices prematurely. Rather than pressuring students to make a choice to meet bureaucratic requirements, colleges need to provide the climate and the services necessary to help students explore a variety of alternatives in an orderly way (Krupa & Vener, 1978).

Students who are in the process of changing their major need the same type of help as those who prefer to be undeclared. They need information about the requirements in new majors and the career implications of these alternatives. They may need help in assessing their abilities for succeeding in a new major.

Academic advisers should have a clear procedure to follow when students decide to change major. They can help students think through the reasons for wanting to change. Referral to the proper resource for help is critical at this point. A combination of services is needed. Students not only need academic information but may need to be referred to a professional career counselor as well.

Research data suggest that unsuccessful attempts to settle on a major or to formulate clear career goals may be factors in attrition (Abel, 1966; Rose & Elton, 1971). More research is needed to help identify who the major-changers are, when help is best, and what type of help is most effective. Rather than leaving these things to chance, organized, creative approaches need to be initiated for helping such a large and needy group.

Undecided Upperclassmen

A few students reach their junior year with no clear career or academic major decision. These students fall into several categories:

Multiplistic Students

Some students, even though they have been able to try out their ideas about a college major through course work and other experiences, still find it difficult to narrow down their choices. All their alternatives seem equally possible and realistic in regard to aptitudes and accessible careers. Most colleges or universities require a decision about a major by the junior year, and so the student is literally forced to make a choice.

When advising advanced undecided students with many areas of interest, a firmer, more confrontive approach is needed. Discussions center around what majors must be "given up" or how to combine several alternatives into one.

Most students, when faced with a forced choice, decide on one alternative with the knowledge that it can be changed later. This knowledge sometimes helps students to commit themselves, since the pressure of making a wrong decision is somewhat dissipated. In the end many students find their tentative choice is a satisfying one and stay with it.

Indecisive Students

The extreme case of a student who is not able to decide is the one whom Goodstein (1965) describes as *indecisive*. A few advanced students need in-depth counseling for a more generalized problem when they cannot make a choice. Indecisive students often have trouble making decisions in many areas of life. High levels of anxiety associated with personal or social conflicts are debilitating. Even though all information is known about possible, realistic alternatives, the indecisive student is still unable to make a commitment.

Hartman and Fuqua (1983) describe students who are chronically undecided due to serious psychological problems. Some students not only find that anxiety associated with indecision impairs their progress but also are too externally controlled or experience identity confusion. Hartman and Fuqua stress the multidimensional nature of indecision and discuss the need for more research to determine other psychological antecedents associated with it. Appropriate interventions need to be developed to help students who are undecided due to these psychological dysfunctions.

It is important to recognize that these few students need counseling help beyond the expertise of most academic advisers. Crites (1981) suggests that even though the surface problem may be career related, a few clients need personal counseling and may find a personality change a desirable counseling outcome. Career decision problems may be resolved once the psychological problems are dealt with.

The New Undecided

Some students who enter college decided about a college major find in time that their original choices are thwarted. This may be due to poor academic performance in selective admissions areas such as the health professions or in popular, oversubscribed majors in which certain grade levels must be maintained. Some academic areas have in recent years seen such an influx of students that they are unable to handle the increased numbers because of limited faculty and other resources. Academic areas such as engineering and business administration (particularly computer science departments) have controlled their enrollments because of these limited resources. Some students are thus in this dilemma because of external circumstances and not by their own choosing. Many formerly decided students are in need of the same resources as undecided ones at this point since they now need to generate other alternatives.

The new undecided students, like the major-changers described earlier, need special approaches. They may need help in resetting goals. They need to identify new options open to them based on their interests and academic record. Workshops offering information about academic majors similar to their original choice provide the information and counseling that is critical during this somewhat difficult transition.

Immature Students

A few upperclassmen still are not ready developmentally to make a choice. They have limited exposure to exploration courses, leisure time activities, or work experiences. They are not motivated to gather information. These students need to be encouraged continually to explore academic alternatives so as to prevent their arriving at their junior year without receiving any organized help or direction.

Crites (1981) suggests that the outcome of developmental counseling should be centered on the progression from orientation and readiness to decision making and reality testing. Chapter 4 discusses the developmental approach in working with undecided students. The immature upperclassman who has not reached a decision about a college major may need to be referred for career counseling.

The above categories are offered not as distinct types of undecided students but as possible reasons for their indecision. Some students reflect many of these characteristics. For example, a junior who has not reached a decision may be slower in personal development, be very anxious about a choice and procrastinate for this reason, and have trouble narrowing down because of many interests. Another group of students are those who are either too lazy or too busy to take the time to put into action a decision that they have already made.

Special Category Undecided Students

In addition to freshmen who enter college undecided and students who change their major, other groups of undecided students require special advising approaches. Although like the others they are uncertain about an educational or career direction, these groups present an additional challenge because of their differing needs.

Undecided Honor Students

Perrone, Malex, and Karshner (1977) identify some career development concerns unique to gifted students: (1) They are told at an early age that they are capable of succeeding in any career and may avoid testing their true competencies because of fear of failure or avoidance of success (Stroup & Jasnosk, 1977; Zaffrann & Colengelo, 1977). (2) Since they receive so much reinforcement they may find it more difficult to measure up to such high expectations. (3) They tend to foreclose too early on a career choice based solely on recognition and success in a particular academic field. (4) Their career interests and values need to be based on a wide range of experiences that are not usually part of the school curriculum. (5) Talented individuals often experience conflict between achieving excellence and being normal. (6) Talented people may become lifelong students because the role is comfortable. (7) Talented students may view a career as their principal means of self-expression and worth.

Hoyt and Hebeler (1974) identify many of the same career choice problems and needs. Multipotentiality presents a dilemma for gifted students since it carries beyond intellectual ability. Bright students often engage in a wide variety of social, athletic, and community activities. Since multipotentiality is a characteristic of most gifted students, selection of careers cannot be based on interests and abilities alone.

Gordon (1983) finds that undecided honors students are less decided about a college major than regular undecided students, less certain of their alternatives, and more uncomfortable during their first quarter. They perform better academically, however, during their freshman year. Moderate levels of discontinuity between students and their college environment enhance personal growth more than either very high or low levels of discontinuity (Feldman & Newcomb, 1969; Pierce, 1970). It would seem that a certain amount of anxiety and uncomfortableness motivate these bright students to achieve at higher levels. While *very* undecided nonhonors student do not perform as well academically as *tentatively* decided nonhonors students, the degree of indecision has no effect on honors students.

Many undecided honors students are interested in areas for which graduate or professional study is required (Hoyt & Hebeler, 1974; Rothney & Sanborn, 1967). This means that advisers need to be familiar with these prerequisites in addition to regular academic information. A generalist adviser with knowledge of related career opportunities can be very helpful as bright undecided students begin to explore many options.

Value clarification techniques are especially useful in advising undecided honors students since these individuals are capable of and have interests in many directions. Helping students clarify and prioritize their values is an important part of the sorting-out process that needs to be accomplished. Gifted honors students often need help in "giving away" some of their alternatives rather than generating additional ones. They can also be helped to identify combinations of several interest areas. Often, combining several interests leads to an entirely new, more satisfying alternative that had not previously been considered. Creating their own major is another option that has appeal to many honors students.

Undecided honors students not only need time to explore but also need to learn to be flexible in making and implementing decisions, since in the future many tire of their vocation and want to change in order to be challenged anew. They also need to learn how to satisfy their other interests through nonvocational activities.

Undecided Student Athletes

Academic opportunities are a consideration when student athletes are recruited. While a few enroll in college initially to further their careers as professional athletes, many others view the college degree as important to their future outside sports. It appears, however, that college athletes who are under great pressure have increased anxiety and high attrition rates (Spandy, 1970; Tutko, 1971). Undecided student athletes with no clear-cut educational or vocational goals are at even higher risk than those who have selected a major.

Spandy (1970) finds that some high school athletes receive personal recognition in their peer group because of their athletic participation. Since this success lies outside the academic structure, student athletes often view college as a largely nonacademic experience. This recognition is continued as students are recruited and become involved in college sports. When educational aspirations remain lower in priority than perceptions of status and recognition, the student athlete does not set realistic educational or vocational goals.

Nelson (1982) finds that athletes who experience a career-counseling group their first semester in college have higher grade point averages and change major more frequently but express higher satisfaction with the major they choose. Changing from undeclared to a major, from major to major, or from a major to being undeclared occurs more frequently among the athletes who experience the career-counseling sessions. Nelson attributes this to the fact that these student athletes are able to assess their personal characteristics in an orderly, structured way and are able to integrate realistically the new occupational and job market information they acquire through the course.

Athletes in general are found to have poorer academic skills and study habits than nonathletes. Some do not develop intellectual self-concepts that are needed to succeed in college (Ewing, 1976; Landers et al., 1978). Sowa and Gressard (1983) find that the overall achievement of athletes is no different from that of nonathletes. They find, however, that athletes have more difficulty formulating educational and career goals than do nonathletes.

These and other findings carry important implications for advising undecided student athletes. Intercollegiate athletes who have unrealistic career goals and aspirations and lower levels of persistence to graduation need academic and career-counseling support throughout their college years.

The time and energy needed for exploration is often a problem since, in addition to being a full-time student, the student athlete spends a significant amount of time in practice and participation in his or her sport. This means that exploration must be accomplished when athletic participation is at a lower level. Course work is an important vehicle for experimentation and exploration. Careful scheduling can help the student athlete experience a variety of academic options while fulfilling the general college requirements.

Helping student athletes set realistic and personally satisfying educational goals can be an extremely critical advising function. Monitoring the student's academic progress is important not only for maintaining athletic eligibility but also for the individual student's academic success and satisfaction throughout the college years.

Adult Undecided Students

An often overlooked population is older returning students, many of whom reenter college for retraining for a specific career or to change their career direction. Many adults, particularly older women, enroll in higher education in order to renew career efforts that were interrupted earlier or to pursue a degree for the sake of receiving a broad education. Not all older students enroll in college with clear-cut educational or vocational goals.

Undecided adult students present a different challenge than traditional-aged students. They offer a set of life experiences and circumstances that must be taken into account as they begin the exploration process. Most older students have a realistic view of their capabilities and their interests. They are often unsure, however, of the academic opportunities available to them. They have had practice and experience with the decision-making process and are usually motivated to seek information actively in an organized way.

Many adults experience apprehension when returning to college. Some feel that being undecided is a temporary state that they must alleviate quickly. Others feel anxious about a decision as they test their abilities to perform college-level work. Adults returning to college may be viewed as developing individuals undergoing change. Adults in particular need support during this period of exploration.

The following describe some special considerations when advising undecided older adult students:

1. Their life experiences and the broader perspective of their life history can be an asset in helping adults identify and explore alternatives. They may have narrowed down many

choices since they are more familiar with their strengths and limitations and what is of interest to them.

2. Adults often present a sense of urgency to make a decision since they feel the need to make up "lost" time. While this can be motivating, it may also work against them, since they may become discouraged in projecting the time it takes to complete an education. Being undecided may be perceived by them (though this is not necessarily true) as a time extender.

3. Adults need to see the relevance of what they are learning and need to be able to apply what they learn immediately. Helping undecided adults access the resources for gathering information and process the information in a personal frame of reference is the type of assistance they need to make a realistic, satisfying educational decision.

4. Older adults feel hesitant to ask for advising help since they feel they are "off time" (Neugarten, Moore & Lowe, 1965). They need assurances that what they are experiencing is a natural part of personal and intellectual development. They need to know that such anxieties are felt by many other older students experiencing the same type of change. The support of a counselor or advisor at this juncture can be critical.

Underprepared Undecided Students

Perhaps the most challenging group of undecided students is those who have poor academic backgrounds. Students who underachieve or who lack the skills to perform a certain level of academic work place great limitations on the areas they may realistically explore. Ashby, Wall, and Osipow (1966) find that academically poor students are actually more decided than their more capable peers. Being decided may offer a certain sense of security as underprepared students enter college.

For working with academically underprepared students, the following considerations are offered:

1. Advisers must be careful not to discourage students prematurely in eliminating alternatives perceived by the adviser to be unrealistic. An underprepared freshman must be given

the time and opportunity to overcome certain academic deficiencies.

2. Advisers must help students deal with academic deficits before emphasizing major exploration. Students must be able to set their priorities in order. Learning how to be a successful student is where initial energies must be concentrated.

3. Upperclassmen who are in academic difficulty sometimes need help in reassessing their original goals and identifying alternatives in which they are more apt to succeed. Advisers must be well trained in alternative counseling since many academically poor students need to change their major. Often, changing from an unrealistic major helps a student out of academic difficulty (as in the case of a premed major who receives excellent grades in social sciences but fails chemistry, math, or physics).

4. As a last resort, decided and undecided academically deficient students may need to be counseled out of college or into a different level or type of educational program. Before that happens, these students deserve educational and career advising that helps them realistically set goals that reflect their potential.

Summary

Many campuses narrowly define *undecided students* as those who enter their institutions openly admitting to a lack of major choice. There are multiple subgroups within the undecided population, each with special characteristics and needs. The undecided entering freshmen can be identified and provided services immediately, and orderly programs for helping them explore can be established.

A larger and often neglected group is the students who enter college ostensibly decided but who become less certain of their choice over time. Students who change their major often need special opportunities for information gathering, self-assessment, and counseling as they proceed through a sometimes difficult transition period. Undecided upperclassmen also comprise a unique group with special needs. Other special categories of undecided students, such as honors, adults, athletes, and underprepared students, have special needs that dictate different approaches to programming and advising.

Each institution needs to obtain a profile of the types and numbers of undecided students on its campus in order to identify the types of programs and services that are needed. Counselors and advisers working with undecided students must be sensitive to the uniqueness of each group and gear their advising approaches accordingly. At any given time, a majority of college students are in some state of doubt or indecision about their educational and career goals. Many students need a carefully organized plan in order to explore. Others need help in confirming a decision that they have already made. A very few may have debilitating psychological problems; their indecision is only a symptom of a more serious dysfunction. All students may be considered unique, developing individuals with very different needs and concerns but with a common need for exploration and decision making.

REFERENCES

Abel, W. H. Attrition and the student who is uncertain. *Personnel and Guidance Journal*, 1966, *44*, 1042–1045.

Ashby, J., Wall, H., and Osipow, C. Vocational uncertainty and indecision in college freshmen. *Personnel and Guidance Journal*, 1966, *44*, 1037–1041.

Beal, P. E., and Noel, L. *What Works in Student Retention.* Iowa City: American College Testing Program and the National Center for Higher Education Management Systems, 1980.

Carney, C. *Psychological Dimensions of Career Development.* Paper presented at a training conference for the Ohio Department of Education, Columbus, Ohio, April, 1975.

Chase, C., and Keene, J. Major declaration and academic motivation. *Journal of College Student Personnel*, 1981, *22*, 496–501.

Cope, R. G., and Hannah, W. *Revolving College Doors.* New York: Wiley, 1975.

Crites, J. O. *Career Counseling: Models, Methods and Materials*, New York: McGraw-Hill, 1981.

Ewing, L. E. Career development of college athletes: Implications for counseling activities. *Dissertation Abstracts*, 1976, *36*, 7204.

Feldman, K., and Newcomb, T. *The Impact of College on Students.* San Francisco: Jossey-Bass, 1969.

Foote, B. Determined-and-undetermined major students: How different are they? *Journal of College Student Personnel*, 1980, *21*, 29–34.

Ginzberg, E. Toward a theory of occupational choice: A restatement. *Vocational Guidance Quarterly*, 1972, *20*, 169–176.

Goodson, W. Do career development needs exist for all students entering colleges or just the undecided major students? *Journal of College Student Personnel*, 1981, *22*, 413–417.

Goodstein, L. Behavior theoretical views of counseling. In B. Steffre (Ed.), *Theories of Counseling*. New York: McGraw-Hill, 1965, pp. 140–192.

Gordon, V. N. The undecided student: A developmental perspective. *Personnel and Guidance Journal*, 1981, *59*, 433–439.

————. Meeting the career development needs of undecided honors students. *Journal of College Student Personnel*, 1983, *24*, 82–83.

Hartman, B., and Fuqua, D. Career indecision from a multidimensional perspective: A reply to Grites. *The School Counselor*, 1983, *30*, 340–346.

Hofman, E., and Grande, P. Academic advising: Matching student's career skills and interests. In E. Watkins (Ed.), *Preparing Liberal Arts Students for Careers*. San Francisco: Jossey-Bass, 1979, pp. 35–47.

Holland, J. L., Daiger, D., and Power, P. *My Vocational Situation*. Palo Alto, California: Consulting Psychologists Press, 1977.

Hoyt, K. B., and Hebeler, J. R. *Career Education for Gifted and Talented Students*. Salt Lake City: Olympus, 1974.

Kojaku, L. Major field transfer: The self-matching of university undergraduates to student characteristics. Los Angeles: UCLA, 1971. (ERIC Document Reproduction Service No. ED 062-933)

Krupa, L., and Vener, A. Career education and the university: A faculty perspective. *Personnel and Guidance Journal*, 1978, *57*, 112–114.

Landers, D., Feltz, D., Obermeier, G., and Brouse, T. Socialization via interscholastic athletes: Its effects on educational attainment. *Research Quarterly*, 1978, *49*, 75–83.

Nelson, E. S. The effects of career counseling of freshmen college athletes. *Journal of Sport Psychology*, 1982, *4*, 32–40.

Neugarten, B., Moore, J., and Lowe, J. Age norms, age constraints, and adult socialization. *American Journal of Sociology*, 1965, *70*, 710–717.

Osipow, S. H., Carney, C., Winer, J., Yanico, B., and Koschier, M. *Career Decision Scale* (3rd revision). Columbus, Ohio: Marathon Consulting and Press, 1976.

Perrone, P., Malex, R., and Karshner, W. Career development needs of talented students: A perspective for counselors. *The School Counselor*, 1977, *27*, 16–23.

Pierce, R. A. Roommate satisfaction as a function of need similarity. *Journal of College Student Personnel*, 1970, *11*, 355–359.

Rose, H., and Elton, C. Attrition and the vocationally undecided student. *Journal of Vocational Behavior*, 1971, *1*, 99–103.

Rothney, J., and Sanborn, M. S. *Identifying and Educating Superior Students in Wisconsin High Schools*. Madison: University of Wisconsin Press, 1967.

Slaney, R. Expressed vocational choice and vocational indecision. *Journal of Counseling Psychology*, 1980, *27*, 122–129.

Sowa, J., and Gressard, C. Athletic participation: Its relationship to student development. *Journal of College Student Personnel*, 1983, *24*, 236–239.

Spandy, W. G. Lament for the letterman: Effects of peer status and extracurricular activities on goals and achievement. *American Journal of Sociology*, 1970, *75*, 680–702.

Stroup, K., and Jasnosk, M. *Do Talented Women Fear Math?* Washington, D.C.: American Association of University Women, 1977. (ERIC Document Reproduction Service No. ED 174395).

Super, D., Starishevsky, R., Matlin, N., and Jordaan, J. *Career Development: Self-Concept Theory.* New York: College Entrance Examination Board, 1963.

Tiedeman, D., and O'Hara, R. *Career Development: Choice and Adjustment.* New York: College Entrance Examination Board, 1963.

Titley, R., and Titley, B. Initial choice of college major: Are only the "undecided" undecided? *Journal of College Student Personnel*, 1980, *8*, 105–111.

Titley, R., Titley, B., and Wolf, W. The major changers: Continuity and discontinuity in the career process: *Journal of Vocational Behavior*, 1976, *8*, 105–111.

Tutko, T. A. Anxiety. In *Encyclopedia of Sport Science and Medicine.* New York: Macmillan, 1971.

Zaffrann, R., and Colengelo, N. Counseling the gifted and talented student. *Gifted Child Quarterly*, 1977, *21*, 305–325.

Chapter 4

A DEVELOPMENTAL ADVISING APPROACH
TO UNDECIDED STUDENTS

Although vocational psychologists have considered indecision a problem in the past, the developmental approach to understanding college students in general and the undecided group in particular is growing in acceptance and support. If entering college students are thought of as developing, maturing adults with specific psychosocial and cognitive tasks to accomplish, the programs and services offered to undecided students take on specific content, sequence, and timing. From this perspective many so-called vocational problems emerge as normal developmental tasks that are resolved at varying times and rates among students during the college years.

A developmental approach to the academic and career advising of undecided students acknowledges the differing characteristics, needs, and rate of maturation unique to each student. Undecided students are viewed *not* as individuals searching for an academic or career niche but as persons continually engaged in a series of developmental tasks that ultimately enable them to adapt and change in a pluralistic world. Thus the scope, variety, and timing of program elements and services for undecided students must incorporate both student and career development concepts and principles (Gordon, 1981). Some of these tenets and how they relate to undecided students are as follows:

1. ALL HUMAN BEINGS DEVELOP THROUGH A LIFE CYCLE THAT HAS CONTINUITY AND FORM. Historical as well as recent research in this area provides an increased awareness and respect for the continuous psychological, social, and physical development of individuals of all ages (Buehler, 1962; Erikson, 1968; Havighurst, 1972).

Implications for Undecided Students — Since individuals develop at their own unique pace and level, undecided students cannot be easily grouped as a whole, or sweeping generalizations made about them. While past research has identified characteristics they seemingly have in common, some of the evidence may be questioned on the basis of limited samples, uncontrolled external variables, and the inconsistencies of the populations being examined. However, a few generalizations about the stages and tasks that undecided students confront are possible. This means that the services offered should be based on the students' needs and not institutional requirements or traditional methods for doing things.

2. DEVELOPMENT IS STAGE AND TASK RELATED. Super et al. (1963) describe life/career development stages and the developmental tasks associated with each stage. Chickering (1969) describes seven psychosocial tasks or vectors that students need to resolve during the college years. He considers these tasks sequential and cumulative. Perry (1970) views the cognitive and moral development of college students in stages; they move from a closed, dualistic perspective to a more open, relativistic one.

Implications for Undecided Students — Thinking of development as stage and task related is particularly relevant to understanding undecided students. The issue of career maturity, including a readiness to commit to an academic or career choice, is crucial to understanding this population. Many undecided students (and indeed many decided ones) are not ready developmentally to make important career and life decisions at eighteen years of age. According to Chickering, students at this age are more concerned with developing physical and social competencies, establishing interpersonal relationships, and finding emotional independence. Career choice implies that issues of identity have been resolved and that a sense of purpose and integrity has been developed to a certain level. Identifying and personalizing values are integral parts of career selection and satisfaction. Perry (1970) describes many freshmen as dualistic, unable to analyze cognitively and synthesize the personal and occupational information necessary to career decision making. Yet, freshmen are expected to commit themselves to a career field with superficial information and limited experience in the real work world.

3. CERTAIN DEVELOPMENTAL TASKS ARE MORE DOMINANT AT CERTAIN STAGES IN THE LIFE CYCLE THAN OTHERS. College students must accomplish certain tasks if they are to be well adjusted in later life. Learning the career choice *process*, for example, is more important for a freshman than making the choice of major or career itself. Confronting identity issues in college is better than trying to resolve problems of social competency and autonomy in midlife.

Implications for Undecided Students — Traditional-aged college students deal with developmental tasks unique to the eighteen– to twenty-three-year-old. According to Chickering, a few of these tasks are establishing independence, developing intellectual competence, learning to manage their body more effectively, learning to manage emotions relating to sex and aggression, and becoming more self-directed and interdependent. College personnel working with older adult students recognize in these students other developmental issues, as well as a reexamination of some of the old ones. Adults returning to college are often searching for new meaning in their lives, prioritizing their values in new and different ways, or looking for new career challenges. Career development tasks are often age related. An undecided student at eighteen is approaching the career decision-making process from a very different perspective than an undecided homemaker returning to college after a twenty-year hiatus.

4. DEVELOPMENTAL TASKS PROGRESS FROM THE SIMPLE TO THE INCREASINGLY COMPLEX (Sanford, 1962). Chickering identifies cycles of differentiation and integration of developmental tasks. As students assimilate new knowledge and learn new behaviors, they must integrate them with existing knowledge and patterns, so that they may function successfully at more complex and appropriate levels of thought and behavior.

Implications for Undecided Students — The programs and services offered undecided students must reflect many levels of ability to differentiate and integrate aspects of the decision-making process. When students are gathering information, for example, the adviser often makes assumptions about their research and interviewing skills. Before sending students out to collect information about major alternatives, the adviser must make sure they have the ability to accomplish such a task. A dualistic student may be searching for the "right" major and be unable to compare and contrast a variety of academic fields. This may lead to discouragement and frustration. The adviser must be sensitive to the level of complexity that particular students are able to tolerate, to recognize where they are in the process and begin the intervention at that level.

5. MANY DEVELOPMENTAL TASKS ARE INTERRELATED AND ARE DEALT WITH SIMULTANEOUSLY. When students enter college they are concerned with being accepted by a new peer group and coping with new academic demands and with pressures related to educational decisions. Developing social competence and succeeding academically have great impact on the career options that are open and realistic for a given student. Personal, social, and career concerns are interrelated at different times during the college years. The levels of intensity concerning these issues vary as well.

Implications for Undecided Students—Some undecided students feel pressured to make a choice of major when they arrive on campus. They are so occupied with other adjustment concerns and personal or academic issues, however, that major exploration often becomes a lower priority. Some students drift during their freshman year and do not explore majors in an orderly way because they are so preoccupied with the other tasks at hand. A developmental program geared to the undecided student should acknowledge their involvement with other tasks and help them integrate these tasks into major and career exploration.

A developmental advising program recognizes that an environment must be created both to challenge and to support students as they risk each forward movement in their personal, academic, and vocational development (Knefelkamp, Widick & Parker, 1978; Perry, 1970). While environmental management is a fairly new concept, it is increasingly recognized as an essential vehicle that ensures that conditions and resources are available to help students grow outside the classroom as well as in it (Crookston, 1972; Harvey, Hunt & Schroder, 1961).

Creating special programs for undecided students is essential if their developmental needs are to be served. The developmental tasks in which students are deeply involved in academic and career decision making are achieving a personal identity, developing a purpose or direction for their life, and learning to identify and personalize their values into a life-style. Although career decisions are made throughout a lifetime, the patterns established during the college years have great impact on how future decisions are approached and resolved.

Career Development Concepts and the Undecided Student

The literature on career development theory and decision making is rife with implications for the undecided student. Several concepts are particularly helpful in understanding the readiness and ability of students to negotiate the decision-making process.

Stages in Decision Making

David Tiedeman and R. O'Hara (1963) describe the decision-making process as comprising a series of tasks that need to be resolved. When people experience discomfort or discontinuities, they initiate purposeful action in the form of decision-making behavior. Tiedeman and O'Hara divide the decision-making process into two phases—planning and action. Students attempting to choose a major or occupation, for example, move through a series of tasks associated with the planning stage. The four planning stages are particularly relevant to understanding the undecided student.

EXPLORATION STAGE. Students at this stage have a vague anxiety about the future. Often they are not aware that there is an orderly process for exploration and choice; thus, they do not have a plan of action. At this point they have no negative choices. Undecided students in the exploration stage need help identifying their strengths and interests and how these relate to academic programs. They need to be made aware that a process for exploration does exist before they can move on to the crystallization stage.

CRYSTALLIZATION STAGE. At this stage students are progressing toward a choice and are beginning to identify some alternatives. They are now able to weigh the advantages and disadvantages of certain alternatives. They may even have made a tentative choice. They are able to recognize earlier decisions as inappropriate.

These students are making normal progress through the planning phase.

Many undecided student are in the crystallization stage. It is important at this point to provide support while they are testing each alternative. Information resources and opportunities to experience certain academic courses or work environments are crucial at this stage. Firsthand experiences help students crystallize or focus on the elements involved in specific alternative choices.

CHOICE STAGE. Students at the choice stage have made a definite commitment to a particular goal. They feel satisfied with and relieved about their decision. If their choice appears to be realistic, they move on to the clarification stage. If, however, they have not made a choice based on relevant information about the area or their abilities to perform in it, they may find the choice is not viable. Many students enter college at the choice stage without having negotiated the first two stages. Tiedeman and O'Hara view these stages as progressive, but they may also be regressive. Many individuals recycle through these stages at different points in their lives when different career decisions need to be resolved.

CLARIFICATION STAGE. The last stage in the planning cycle is clarification, in which the consequences of choice are internalized. Since a definite commitment has been made, a plan of action can be initiated and implemented. The adviser's obligation to undecided students is to support them through the clarification stage.

The action stages of induction, reformation, and integration occur as the choice is successfully synthesized with the student's image and the decision is integrated into his or her life.

Vincent Harren (1979) provides a career decision-making model based on Tiedeman and O'Hara's assumptions. He identifies four interrelated parameters that specify how the characteristics of the decision-maker, the type of decision, and the milieu in which the decision is made are integrated into the process itself.

Harren postulates a four-stage sequential process for decision making. He begins with an awareness stage, in which individuals become attentive to their situation. If dissatisfaction results, they move into the planning stage. This incorporates the exploration and crystallization stages of Tiedeman and O'Hara's paradigm. Here information is gathered, and alternatives are identified and narrowed. When a specific alternative is settled upon, a transition is made into the commitment stage, in which the decision is integrated into the individual's self-concept system. If the fit is confirmed, there is a transition into the final or implementation stage. At this time the decision is assimilated into the new context unless the individual's needs and values change or external factors affect the decision adversely. If that happens, the individual turns away from implementation and recycles through the process so that other alternatives may be identified and explored.

Harren also incorporates student development concepts into his model. Within the career decision-making process, certain developmental tasks must be resolved. These include autonomy, interpersonal maturity, and development of a sense of purpose. This explains why undecided persons vary in their level of ability to perform the decision-making tasks. The timing of the decision and the maturity of the individual affect his or her readiness and ability to accomplish specific tasks.

Harren's model not only provides an explanation of the progression that students experience in making decisions but also offers a rationale for providing specific advising and career-counseling activities at specific periods in the process of exploration and choosing a major.

Levels of Indecision

A practical application of Tiedeman and O'Hara's concept is understanding the various levels of indecision among individual undecided students. Advising approaches for students who are tentatively decided, for example, can be very different from those for the totally undecided. When undecided students are placed within Tiedeman and O'Hara's planning stages, certain antecedents of indecision may be apparent, and possible advising interventions may be suggested. Students who are completely undecided may be in Tiedeman and O'Hara's exploration stage, in which seemingly no progress is being made. This level is similar to Harren's awareness stage, in which students begin to realize that they need to pay some attention to their situation.

Students who have identified two or more alternatives are making progress and need to gather and organize information about each option. These tentatively decided students are ready to explore and crystallize their alternatives, according to Tiedeman and O'Hara.

Tiedeman and O'Hara's choice stage implies that a decision has been reached, but if the student still has doubts, a real commitment is not made. Students who verbalize their indecision but have internally made a choice often need to reality-test the idea before publically committing to it. While this is a small group, advising approaches to them can be very different. Figure 2 outlines these levels of indecision, and possible causes and interventions for each level are suggested.

When all doubts are satisfied the students moves on to the clarification stage. Here they need help formalizing an action plan so that they may actually perform in the major or career field they have chosen. Harren calls this the implementation stage.

While these stages or levels are theoretical, they facilitate understanding of an orderly progression of becoming decided. There are many levels and types of approaches that may be initiated with a particular student. Some students are ready for information gathering, while others are ready to process the information they already have. Some are developmentally ready to move on to the next set of tasks, while others are not. This is why an individual advising approach to undecided students needs to be in tune with the particular student's stage of readiness and development.

Career Maturity

Another important concept that has implications for advising the undecided student is career maturity. John Crites (1981) lists five stages of career maturation. Undecided students must accomplish these five tasks before they are vocationally mature enough to make a decision:

1. *Orientation to vocational choice:* This implies an awareness of the need to choose and an awareness of the factors involved in choosing a major or occupation.
2. *Information and planning:* This refers to the amount of reliable information an individual possesses with which to make a decision. Students must also learn to plan logically and chronologically for the future.

LEVELS, ANTECEDENTS, AND INTERVENTIONS FOR INDECISION*

Levels of Indecision	Possible Causes or Antecedents	Possible Approaches or Interventions
COMPLETELY UNDECIDED (considering no choice)	Search for one "right" choice Lack of value identity Failure to identify or use known interest patterns Uncertainty about abilities Inability to organize thoughts Narrowing of options due to sex stereotyping No feeling of pressure to move toward decision Resistance of parental/societal pressures to choose Lack of hobbies or extracurricular experiences Void of information about occupations Lack of work experience	Help explore cause of indecision Teach decision-making process Help begin to identify values and interests Provide sex-role identity counseling Provide anxiety counseling Help organize information search Help generate alternatives Dispel myths about career choice Help identify and test abilities and skills Provide personal/social counseling Encourage work/volunteer experiences
TENTATIVELY DECIDED (considering two or more choices)	Multiplicity of interests Value conflict/confusion Inadequate information about alternatives General inability to make decisions Uncertainty about abilities Reluctance to give up any one choice Attempt to please other people	Help clarify values Help organize information on self and occupations Help combine best elements of alternatives into one Provide anxiety counseling Teach decision-making process Force field analysis
UNCOMMITTED DECIDED (choice has been made)	Resistance of outside pressures to declare choice Inadequate information about choice Uncertainty about ability for choice Lack of direct occupational use for educational choice High competition in choice Sex opposition of those in occupation (e.g. males in nursing) Job market known to be poor Inadequate rewards Attempt to please others Fear of being "locked in" to choice	Reach decision-making process Allow time Help acquire more information about choice Help check accuracy of occupational information Provide anxiety counseling Help confirm accuracy of self-information Provide reassurance counseling Help clarify values implicit in choice Help determine life goals

*These are not intended to be inclusive or exclusive. One student's indecision may incorporate a combination of several causes, and many approaches may be used simultaneously or over a period of time.

3. *Crystallization of traits:* This refers to the psychological attributes a person brings to decision making, such as interest patterns, explicit values, and increasing independence. Crystallization requires the ability to bring all the relevant factors together into a coherent whole.
4. *Wisdom of vocational preferences:* This refers to how closely an individual's career decisions agree with various aspects of reality. For example, do they have the prerequisite ability for their preferred occupation, appropriate interests for the chosen field, available financial resources for relevant training, etc.? Is the choice realistic in every way?

Students are often forced by institutions to make decisions at a time when they are not developmentally ready. Developing career maturity is a critical task that needs to be acknowledged and dealt with in individualizing advising approaches for undecided students. The developmental adviser can be extremely helpful in making certain that students are aware of the tasks associated with career decision making and helping them develop the skills necessary to accomplish this process.

Advising Individual Undecided Students

Although many services may be offered, one-to-one advising is still the core of most advising efforts. Adviser and student need to establish the roles and responsibilities of their relationship from the outset. Kramer and Gardner (1983) suggest that an advising contract be drawn up so that these responsibilities can be discussed and clearly stated. Students need to understand the time and energy involved in exploration. They need to acknowledge that the responsibility for exploration is theirs, as well as the responsibility for a decision once it is made.

Adviser's responsibilities include helping students define their goals, helping them assess their personal strengths and limitations, and acting as a resource for information and referral, as well as helping them generate viable alternatives. Advisers can offer the support that students need during the exploration process.

Both adviser and advisee need to determine the outcomes of the exploration process. Too often adviser and student exchange information as though this were the goal of the advising relationship. Students not only need help in gathering information but need help in processing it as well. Self-, academic and career information needs to be integrated in a personal framework. Only then can tentative decisions be reached and action to implement them be taken.

Advisers can teach students decision making by modeling the process during the advising exchange. This means that an orderly progression of tasks needs to be accomplished. These tasks are outlined below.

Task 1: *Help the student determine why he or she is undecided.*

There are as many reasons for being undecided as there are students. Any academic or career adviser working with undecided students quickly discerns the complexity and number of reasons for indecision in individual students. The list below summarizes a few of these causes. An individual student may be involved in more than one of them simultaneously.

- *Lack of independence in decision making*—Some students have had decisions made for them for many years by parents, teachers, and external circumstances. They have never had the opportunity to make decisions for themselves or taken responsibility for decisions once they were made. Some students entering college expect the same patterns to continue. They anticipate that faculty, counselors, or academic advisers will make academic and career decisions for them. They believe that all decisions will come from some force outside themselves.
- *Lack of knowledge of the decision-making process* — Many entering college students are unaware that there is an orderly process for exploring and selecting an academic major or career field. They have made decisions in the past but have rarely stopped to analyze all the factors involved in the process itself. They

tend to approach important decisions such as career and life planning in the same way as insignificant ones. Thus they have no experience upon which to draw when they are confronted with academic and vocational decisions in college.

- *Lack of information* — Very often students have no concrete, realistic information on which to base an educational decision even if they know how to make it. Informational deficits are one of the most common problems among undecided students (and among some decided ones as well). Often students do not know how, where, what, or from whom to collect the information that is so vital to informed educational decisions.

- *Multiplicity of interests* — Some students have so many areas of interest they cannot decide between them. In some cases it takes more detailed information to help them sort out the real differences in their alternatives. For others it is a matter of "giving up" some closely held alternatives. For others it may mean combining several areas of interest into one new alternative.

- *Lack of interests* — On the other end of the continuum are the students who claim they have absolutely no interests at all. Many students have difficulty verbalizing interests even though they have them. This situation is more difficult to overcome than that of students with many interests. Students unable to express their interests may have had very few experiences on which to base an opinion. They may be fearful of uttering an idea aloud since they feel that it may be construed as a commitment. Some may have difficulty expressing themselves about other areas of life as well.

- *Lack of ability* — Some students' interests are in areas in which they have doubts about their abilities to succeed. Some college freshmen do not know their abilities since they have never really tested them. If they exerted a minimum amount of effort in high school, they may doubt their capabilities in some areas. They may not be motivated to take risks or may not be willing to invest the energy required to find out what their abilities are. Others may not know *how* to determine what they are capable of.

- *Lack of knowledge about educational and occupational relationships* —

Many students are concerned about the types of occupations to which a particular major leads. Others have career goals but do not know the majors that will help them attain these goals. These educational and occupational links are perceived as mutually inclusive by some students. Some will not choose an academic major unless it has an obvious relationship with an occupational field. Whether to choose a major or an occupation first is the "chicken and egg" question with which many students struggle. Many decided students make initial choices because this relationship is obvious. This is a particularly difficult issue with students who are inclined toward the liberal arts.

- *Lack of desire to attend college* — Some students are undecided because they do not want to be in college. They enrolled because of outside pressures, but their interests and goals do not include a college degree. They may not feel "ready" to tackle the college environment. They are therefore not motivated even to explore some of the options a particular campus offers.

There are obviously many other reasons for an individual student's indecision. Both Holland and Holland (1977) and Osipow, Carney, and Barak (1976) have developed diagnostic instruments to help adviser and student assess the reasons for indecision. These can be very useful in an initial contact since they can pinpoint concerns in areas of self-identity, informational deficits, or external barriers very quickly. Helping the student identify and verbalize the issues that are involved in his or her situation can be an important first task in the exploration process.

Crites (1981) discusses three diagnostic approaches and the contributions that various counseling models make to the adviser or counselor of undecided students. *Differential diagnosis* tries to determine the student's career decision problems. For example, a student's choice of a major or occupation may require a level of aptitude that he or she does not possess. This makes the choice unrealistic. *Dynamic diagnosis* is concerned with *why* the student cannot decide. The student may be indecisive in most decision-making situations and therefore have difficulty with this one. To determine the developmental context of the decision maker, Crites suggests a *decisional diagnosis*. This takes into consideration the student's career maturity at a given point. The student, for example, may not be able to assess her or his personal strengths objectively. Whatever aspect of career maturity is below average can be identified as a focus for an intervention. The *Career Maturity Inventory* (Crites, 1973) provides information about a student's maturity in the areas of self-appraisal, occupational information, goal selection, planning, problem solving, and attitudes. This is an example of an instrument that can help the adviser and student determine the area or areas on which the student needs to focus.

Other issues to explore with the student during the initial contact are:

- *Determining the level of indecision* — If the student has a tentative idea in mind, he or she requires a more informational approach than a student who is totally undecided, for whom more self-assessment activities might be indicated.
- *Determining the level of commitment to exploring* — How motivated is the student to devote the time and energy necessary to the exploration process? Students who are feeling some discontinuity or anxiety for changing their undecided status become involved in the tasks necessary to reach a decision. Some students may not be ready to choose a major. They may be in Tiedeman and O'Hara's awareness stage and so are not prepared to explore or crystallize a choice. Career maturity may also be a factor here. A plan for gathering information will not be used by a student who feels no need to change the status quo.
- *Exploring personal concerns about being undecided* — An adviser can help a student articulate feelings associated with being undecided. Some students feel eager and ready to explore. Others feel anxious or pressured by parents, friends, or the institution to make a decision. The affective dimension must be acknowledged and dealt with before any serious exploration can take place.
- *Identifying the student's decision-making style* — Some students need to determine how past decision-making experiences

affect their search for alternatives. Has their decision-making style been productive or nonproductive in the past? Do they rely on external forces to decide for them? Who has been involved in their academic and career planning in the past? Are they ready to take responsibility for the decisions they will eventually make?

During this initial phase of individual advising, the adviser needs to establish a supportive, caring climate so that the student feels comfortable in identifying the problem and feels confident that the exploration process will be a positive, productive experience.

Task 2: Help the student organize a plan for exploring.

This is the information-gathering part of the process. Some students need to assess their personal characteristics in depth. Many times this means referring them to a career counselor, a career-planning course for credit, or a testing center. There are many aspects to self-appraisal, and the adviser and student need to determine the extent and depth that are needed. Personality instruments, interest and value inventories, aptitude and ability measures, and decision-making instruments are a few resources that may be used. There is always a danger, however, that students will use these results in a literal translation of what their choice should be. The real value of an interest inventory, for example, is as a starting place for helping the student focus on areas that are (often) being considered anyway. To subject an undecided student to a battery of tests indiscriminately without a rationale or plan may only serve to confuse him or her more. Testing experiences, however, if properly controlled, can help a student integrate a great deal of personal information into a framework in which alternatives may be identified and studied.

Crites (1981) discusses the place of testing in career counseling. He maintains that new modes and methods for using tests make them potentially useful for the student with problems in career selection. Both test and nontest data are needed to clarify the problem, which can then indicate solutions. Accumulating and integrating self-knowledge are critical components of decision making.

Another area of information that is vital to the exploration process pertains to college majors. Many students enter college with limited knowledge of majors, program options, course requirements, and electives. Most advisers are on comfortable ground in this area. Although much information is provided in college catalogs and bulletins, these sometimes do not have an easy format for exploration and are often changeable. Many students need the personal, one-to-one contact that only direct personal interviewing provides.

When gathering information about academic programs, undecided students need—

1. *to begin with, a general overview of all majors offered on a campus.* This introduces them to programs they may not know exist and places parameters on all possible options. Knowing the outside limits of possible choices is often revealing to a student who does not know where to start.

2. *a summary of the basic requirements for all majors.* This reveals all the common course requirements across the areas being considered. The summary also aids students in scheduling courses that overlap all the majors of interest to them. Scheduling in this way keeps options open while the exploration process is in progress.

3. *help in generating a list of questions to ask faculty, college counselors, and other resource persons,* so that when informational contacts are made their questions will be organized and relevant. Teaching interviewing skills helps students become more confident in this important aspect of exploring.

4. *the opportunity to share information and reflect on it with a generalist adviser.* The advantages and disadvantages of each possibility can be weighed and discussed. This is a very important step in the information-gathering phase of exploration. An adviser can serve an important function here—to listen, question, and help students reflect on the information collected.

Another informational area concerns occupations and job market projections. This is a complex body of knowledge and one that changes rapidly. Since advisers cannot be expected to become experts in this area, other campus resources must provide students the opportunity to be exposed to this information. The usual sources are faculty in specific fields, placement offices, and career libraries. Since this search can be overwhelming for students, a classification system needs to be available to help them translate their interests, abilities, academic major interests, and other personal data into occupational groups. Examples of systems for organizing occupational information into usable formats are the Career Decision-Making Program developed by the Appalachia Educational Laboratory (AEL; 1978), published by McKnight Publishers, the Holland (1973) system, and the Career Family classification developed by the American College Testing (ACT) Program (1972). The AEL system uses the Department of Labor's Worker Trait Group occupational classification, and the Holland system is based on John Holland's theory of personality in careers. ACT organizes occupations into twelve job families.

Another important resource is the computerized career information systems such as DISCOVER (1982), SIGI (1980), and CHOICES (1980). These systems are currently the best resources for accessing vast, current occupational and job market information, since they are updated every year.

One danger in the information-gathering task is the possibility of overwhelming students with an overload in a short period of time. Information gathering needs to take place over a period of time with frequent breaks for reflection and thought. Too much information too quickly only confuses some students and makes them feel even more pressured and bewildered. Advisers need to help students pace themselves in keeping with their individual ability to gather and assimilate information in a productive way.

Task 3: Help the student integrate all the information that has been collected.

This is the step that many students find very difficult. Gathering information can be a very positive experience, but pulling it all together into meaningful, manageable form can be overwhelming for some students. This is why each student's level of maturity and development is important to ascertain. A dualistic student, for example, may still be looking for the right and only choice and thus not be able to integrate or synthesize the information that has been obtained.

Advisers can help students generate or confirm realistic alternatives from the data that have been collected. Students need to see relationships between their personal strengths and certain academic major options. Occupational implications clearly influence many students' choices, since finding a career is a reason they give for being in college. Helping students determine these relationships may be the most important task of an adviser. This can be a vital learning experience for many students.

The computerized career information systems mentioned above are extremely useful in helping students integrate information about self, majors, and occupations. Many students find these systems not only help them access information in an organized, readily understandable form but also help them integrate it in a very personal decision-making framework.

Task 4: Support the student while he or she makes decisions.

It is obvious that students alone must make final academic and career decisions, but they may need support, as they sometimes struggle with making a commitment to a choice. This is why understanding the individual student's decision-making background and style is important. Some students reach this point and find they need to return to the information-gathering task if no alternative emerges. Others are hesitant to make a decision because of lack of confidence in their ability to do so. Other students find external forces negate a specific alternative (for example, lack of financial support for entering a professional college such as medicine).

Advisers need to encourage students to return for discussion if the need arises as the student finally selects a major choice. Many students find the personal support of a caring adult reassuring at this stage.

Task 5: *Help the student initiate an action plan.*

Making a decision is only the beginning. A carefully considered plan for implementing the choice must also be initiated. Many students feel a great sense of relief after a decision is reached. Advisers can—

- help students outline an action plan that specifies the activities to be done and the time frame in which these need to be accomplished.
- point out short– and long-term action steps that need to be in sequence.
- help students realize that plans need to be periodically reevaluated and changed as new information or circumstances indicate.

Task 6: *Encourage follow-up contact.*

Advisers need to make it clear to students that they are always available for future discussions. Making a major decision and implementing it are important accomplishments for many students. Knowing that an interested, caring adult is available can be reassuring as they live out the decision they have made.

Not all students progress through this process in an orderly way. Some may not be ready to finalize a decision and may stop their search at an earlier point. When adviser and student can formulate a plan for exploration that is clearly defined and personalized, however, the outcome is usually satisfying.

Summary

Undecided students may be viewed as striving, maturing individuals who are in various stages of personal and career development. Career maturity implies an awareness and readiness to tackle the tasks that are necessary to the decision-making process. Each student approaches these tasks in a very personalized and unique manner. Developmental advising implies that each student's individual needs are recognized and incorporated into the exploration process.

Undecided students can be taught the decision-making process.

Exploration of various alternatives and crystallization of these options must precede the actual choice. Specific steps are outlined for the advising relationship, including identifying the reasons for the student's indecision, gathering information, integrating the information once it is collected, and providing support while the student is making a commitment to a specific choice. Once a decision is made, many students require assistance in formulating and carrying out a plan of action.

REFERENCES

American College Testing Program. *Career Family List*. Iowa City: American College Testing Program, 1982.

Appalachia Educational Laboratory. *Career Decision Making Program*. Bloomington, Illinois: McKnight, 1978.

Buehler, C. Genetic aspects of the self. *Annals of the New York Academy of Sciences*, 1962, *96*, 730–764.

Chickering, A. W. *Education and Identity*. San Francisco: Jossey-Bass, 1969.

Chickering, A. W., and associates. *The Modern American College*. San Francisco: Jossey-Bass, 1981.

CHOICES. Ottowa, Ontario: Occupational and Career Analysis and Development, 1980.

Crites, J. O. *Theory and Research Handbook for the Career Maturity Inventory*. Monterey, California: CTB/McGraw-Hill, 1973.

_____. *Career Counseling: Models, Methods, and Materials*. New York: McGraw-Hill, 1981.

Crookston, B. B. A developmental view of academic advising as teaching. *Journal of College Student Personnel*, 1972, *13*, 12–17.

DISCOVER. Hunt Valley, Maryland: American College Testing Program, 1982.

Erikson, E. *Identity: Youth and Crises*. New York: Norton, 1968.

Gordon, V. N. The undecided student: A developmental perspective. *Personnel and Guidance Journal*, 1981, *59*, 433–439.

Harren, V. A model of career decision making for college students. *Journal of Vocational Behavior*, 1979, *14*, 119–133.

Harvey, O., Hunt, D., and Schroder, H. *Conceptual Systems and Personality Organizations*. New York: Wiley, 1961.

Havighurst, R. F. *Developmental Tasks and Education* (3rd ed.). New York: McKay, 1972.

Holland, J. L. *Making Vocational Choices: A Theory of Careers*. Englewood Cliffs, N.J.: Prentice-Hall, 1973.

Holland, J. L., and Holland, J. E. Vocational indecision: More evidence and speculation. *Journal of Counseling Psychology*, 1977, *24*, 404–414.

Knefelkamp, L., Widick, C., and Parker, C. (Eds.). *New Directions for Student Services: Applying New Developmental Findings*, No. 4. San Francisco: Jossey-Bass, 1978.

Kramer, H., and Gardner, R. *Advising by Faculty*. Washington, D.C.: National Education Association, 1983.

Osipow, S. W., Carney, C., and Barak, A. A scale of educational-vocational undecidedness. *Journal of Vocational Behavior*, 1976, 9, 233–243.

Perry, W. G., Jr. *Intellectual and Ethical Development in the College Years*. New York: Holt, Rinehart and Winston, 1970.

Sanford, N. (Ed.). *The American College*. New York: Wiley, 1962.

SIGI. Princeton, N.J.: Educational Testing Service, 1980.

Super, D., Starishevsky, R., Matlin, N., and Jordaan, J. *Career Development: Self-Concept Theory*. New York: College Entrance Examination Board, 1963.

Tiedeman, D., and O'Hara, R. *Career Development: Choice and Adjustment*. New York: College Entrance Examination Board, 1963.

Winston, R., Ender, S., and Miller, T. (Eds.). *New Directions for Student Services: Developmental Approaches to Academic Advising*, No. 17. San Francisco: Jossey-Bass, 1982.

Chapter 5

PROGRAM COMPONENTS:
METHODS AND TECHNIQUES

T he comprehensive academic and career advising services required by undecided students imply a variety of program
elements. The scope of services outlined in Chapter 2 may be
implemented through many activities and techniques. Practical
individual and group interventions are described in this chapter.
While some of these services already exist on many campuses,
programmatic emphasis or expansion may be needed to adapt
them to the special needs of the undecided population. Program
components fall into several categories: (1) those pertaining to
individual advising and counseling, (2) those created for group
involvement, and (3) those initiated to improve the expertise and
techniques of advisers or others working with undecided students.

Individual Student Approaches

Although many program components and materials may be
applied to both individuals and groups of students, some are
especially effective for working on a one-to-one basis. Since each
student has a unique set of personal characteristics and decision-
making style, some of these approaches are more applicable to
one type of student than to another. For example, one student may
find a career library or a computer system more conducive to
exploration than does a student who prefers to gather information
by interviewing workers in a career field or participating in a
small-group discussion. Advisers must be able to recognize and
implement different methods and approaches that reflect individual student needs.

TESTING. Many counseling and career centers offer testing

opportunities that can help students become personally involved in self-assessment. A few examples of testing resources are listed below. A description of these instruments and their publishers may be found in a number of resources such as Buros's *Tests in Print (1972)*, *The Eighth Mental Measurement Yearbook* (Buros, 1978), and *Using Assessment Results in Career Counseling*, by Zunker (1982).

INTEREST INVENTORIES. Interest inventories are probably the best known and most widely used of all career self-assessment tools. Their main value is in helping students organize or focus on what they enjoy or like. Interest patterns have been researched extensively for thirty years, and certain patterns are known to be predictive of satisfaction with certain career fields (Campbell, 1974; Kuder, 1963).

There are many familiar inventories such as the *Strong-Campbell Interest Inventory* (SCII), *Ohio Vocational Interest Survey* (OVIS), *Jackson Vocational Interest Survey* (JVIS), *Kuder Occupational Interest Survey — Form DD*, and *ACT Interest Inventory* (UNIACT). Some inventories help students compare their interests with those of workers in a certain career field who are satisfied with their occupations; others help students measure their interests in relationship to tasks performed in the occupation. Since interest inventories can help students relate their interests or what they like with specific groups of occupations, they help build that important bridge between the "Who am I?" question and the work world.

APTITUDE ASSESSMENT. Many students use the terms *achievement, ability,* and *aptitude* interchangeably. *Achievement,* however, can be viewed as a measure of what has already been learned. The American College Test (ACT) and Scholastic Achievement Test (SAT) are examples of this type of assessment. *Abilities* are measured in the present tense — what students know about their strengths and limitations at this point in time. *Aptitudes* are future oriented — what the student's potential is. The *Generalized Aptitude Test Battery* (GATB) and the *Differential Aptitude Test* (DAT) are examples of aptitude tests. The Department of Labor has identified eleven aptitudes that are inherent in all occupations. Students can measure potential for certain careers by assessing their level of aptitude in such areas as verbal and abstract reasoning, numerical reasoning, and spatial or mechanical aptitude. Aptitudes are then related to specific occupational clusters called *Worker Trait Groups.*

VALUE ASSESSMENT. Some students have never questioned what is inherently important to them in a career. Work values such as prestige, money, power, creativity, and independence are implicit in occupations. When students can identify what is of value to them, they can then relate these values to specific occupations. Values can be measured by instruments such as the *Work Values Inventory* (WVI) and the *Temperament and Values Inventory* (*TVI*). Values clarification exercises as outlined in many resources provide another approach (Simon, Howe & Kirschenbaum, 1972).

PERSONALITY INVENTORIES. Many important career theorists (Holland, 1973; Osipow, 1983; Super, 1957) stress the importance of considering personality factors and characteristics in making educational and career decisions. Such personality variables as needs, temperament, anxiety, and extraversion/introversion can be related to occupational groups. The *Omnibus Personality Inventory (OPI), Sixteen Personality Factor Questionnaire (16PF)*, and *Hall Occupational Orientation Inventory (HOOI)* are instruments providing information about students' personality traits, which can be related to careers. The *Myers-Briggs Type Indicator* (MBTI) is used to help students confirm ideas they may have about certain career fields or open up possibilities they had not yet considered (Gordon & Sears, 1983; Myers, 1980; Pinkney, 1983).

While testing is helpful to students in broadening their perceptions of careers and themselves, it is not to be considered an end in itself. It is only one method for gathering information. Some students think the test will tell them what decision to make. Advisers and counselors must be ready to place testing into its proper perspective — as one information source among many.

COUNSELING. Some undecided students need the services of a psychological counselor. If a great deal of anxiety is experienced with the decision-making process, the student may need help alleviating the stress or learning to cope with it. Some identity concerns also require personal counseling. Some students feel controlled by another person or situation and are unable to negotiate the decision-making process because of these external constraints. Counseling can help students develop a more internal locus of control so they can make decisions independently. Some developmental concerns such as social adjustment problems also require individual counseling. Counseling may be needed to alleviate many kinds of temporary concerns that students experience.

Another group of students who are unable to make decisions may have serious psychological dysfunctions (Fuqua & Hartman, 1983; Goodstein, 1965; Hartman & Fuqua, 1983). These students need longer-term psychological counseling. Although there are no reliable diagnostic procedures for identifying these students at present, the number with serious psychological problems is probably small. Psychological services can help students with temporary developmental concerns or with more serious personality dysfunctions. On small campuses this help may need to come from a community mental health center or private practioners.

CAREER LIBRARIES. Many campuses have library facilities organized to help students obtain information about majors and careers. Libraries may be organized according to several classification systems that can help students access this extensive and complex body of information in an orderly way. Three systems that are designed to help students access career information from a personal perspective are:

1. John Holland's classification system (Gottfredson, Holland & Ogawa, 1982), which places occupations into a three-letter code system derived from his six personality types.

2. The job family system in *VIESA*, in which occupations are integrated into categories based on interests, experiences, and values (American College Testing Programs, 1982).

3. The Department of Labor's Worker Trait Group (WTG) System, which is used by the *Career Decision-Making Program* (Appalachia Educational Laboratory, 1978). This system integrates the *Dictionary of Occupational Titles*, the *Occupational Outlook Handbook*, and other government documents into a comprehensive scheme of occupational information that can be accessed from such personal characteristics as work activities and situations, aptitudes, and educational training.

Whichever organizing system is used in a career library (including the simple alphabetical listing of occupations), students need to learn how to use it. This may be accomplished through individual contacts, group workshops, freshman orientation courses, or career-planning courses. Individual students can spend as much time as they wish and learn at their own pace in a career library.

Career libraries must constantly update printed materials if the student is to make decisions based on accurate information. Care must be exercised to maintain information sources that are not unrealistically slanted or biased. For example, sex biases may be hidden in certain information, or company brochures may make generalizations that do not apply to local situations. Career libraries need to be initiated and maintained by professionals who are trained in this area.

COMPUTERIZED INFORMATION SYSTEMS. The most recent and exciting method for accessing personal, academic, and career information is through computerized information systems. Some advantages are:

1. *Computer systems provide a personalized exploration of self.* If students wish to take an interest inventory or an ability measure or to clarify work values, the computer program offers these opportunities in a clear, easy-to-access way.

2. *Voluminous, up-to-date occupational information is offered in an easy-to-understand format.* Many career libraries struggle to keep occupational and job market information current. Computer systems are updated annually based on many sources, including current government, business, and industry data.

3. *Computerized systems are excellent tools for helping students integrate personal and occupational information.* Computer programs can relate students' interests, values, and abilities to specific career fields. The students often can receive a detailed description of these alternatives in a printout.

4. *Computer systems can teach students decision-making strategies.* Some systems have built-in programs for helping students experience the decision-making process itself. Students can simulate a variety of choices without taking the risks associated with real-world decisions. Computer systems are a safe place to practice different decision-making styles and strategies.

5. *Students are in control.* The computerized approach encourages students to be intimately involved in their own career planning. They are not relying on other people's opinions

or wishes. Through different combinations of personal factors they can experience different outcomes.

6. *Computer systems can help students plan for appropriate action.* Once certain decisions are made, students are presented with a list of action steps in some systems. Implementation of a decision becomes more structured and easier to accomplish. Some examples of these systems include DISCOVER, SIGI, CVIS, and CHOICES.

Computerized systems are also being developed as an interactive academic advising tool (Rees & Fischer, 1983). Students may access academic major information such as general and specific course requirements for a degree. Other programs provide information about academic regulations and policies, grading, and special academic opportunities such as honor programs and study abroad.

Computers will never replace advisers, but they can enhance the quality of the one-to-one exchange. The routine part of advising — specific information giving — can be accomplished effectively by computers. This allows the adviser and student to concentrate on personal impressions and applications of that information.

CAREER MODULES. There are many programmed materials that provide students with a structured vehicle for assessing personal characteristics and relating them to occupational fields. The *Self-Directed Search* (Holland, 1977) and *VIESA* (American College Testing Program, 1983) are examples of tools for helping students understand interests and abilities. These modules can also help students integrate self-information and occupational information. An adviser or counselor can use these materials as an initial effort in helping students identify and focus on certain alternatives. These comprehensive, self-contained units are excellent for individual advising or for use in small groups since they are self-scored and results can be obtained immediately.

COMMUNITY RESOURCES. An invaluable source of information for undecided students is the worker in the field. Some campuses have established lists composed of graduates of the institution who have volunteered to discuss their occupational field with exploring students. This personal contact has several advantages. It provides students with the names of individuals who are willing to talk to them about a field in which they have an interest. Discussing accounting with two or three accountants working in different settings can broaden a student's perception of what the work really entails. The student may discuss this occupation with the alumni on the telephone or by actually visiting the work environment for a day or longer. This program also has the advantage of involving alumni in their alma mater's mission beyond the usual fund-giving activity.

Some students are able to receive course credit for actual work experiences on some campuses. Spending a school term in a school, a hospital, a social agency, or a business, for example, provides the type and depth of information students need in order to make informed choices. Experiencing programs may be organized with the help of the alumni office or with community leaders and business personnel. A list of volunteer work sites is another method for providing the experience opportunity to undecided students.

Some institutions have co-op or intern programs, in which students can get practical experience in a particular work environment, usually for pay. Many campuses have federally funded programs for co-op experiences.

Programs for Group Advising

While a great deal of advising is geared to individual contact, group activities have several advantages. Providing information to small groups of students is a more efficient use of time, since many students may be served with one effort. Groups also provide an opportunity for students to share common concerns. When undecided students realize they are experiencing many of the same problems as their peers, they may not feel as isolated or different.

WORKSHOPS. Small-group activities such as workshops can be provided on many topical areas. A workshop format may include, for example, test taking and interpretation, which can be an effective beginning to self-assessment. Decision-making skills may be taught in a workshop. Other examples of workshop topics include values and careers, sex-role identity and careers, an overview of academic majors, academic major alternatives, the job outlook, careers in business (or engineering, health fields, psychology, etc.). Workshop subject matter is unlimited when the need for information and academic counseling is considered.

Programmed career modules also lend themselves to group activity since students can work through the exploration process in a structured way and can immediately share results with peers and counselors. There are many commercial products available, but they may be developed locally as well.

FRESHMAN ORIENTATION COURSES. The need for an extension of the normally brief precollege orientation is well known. The first freshman seminar course was taught in the late 1800s, and by 1925 over 100 institutions offered such courses (Fitts & Swift, 1928). The purpose of most freshman orientation courses is to support and provide information to new students during their first weeks in college. Designing a course format especially for undecided students has many advantages:

1. *Undecided students receive immediate individual attention.* They are provided with help in gathering information or adjusting to college when they need it most. The class provides a support group during their initial contact with the campus environment.
2. *The instructor may be the student's academic adviser.* If adviser assignments are made in this way, regular contact is established; adviser and student can begin to form a working relationship immediately.
3. *Immediate adjustment concerns are identified and resolved.* Students with poor study habits, for example, can learn how to improve them during the freshman orientation course.
4. *Self-assessment is provided in a structured way.* Self-information can be collected, organized, and processed immediately.
5. *Academic major information is provided in depth.* The student is offered breadth and depth of information that would otherwise take a great deal of time and motivation to gather individually.
6. *Educational and occupational relationships are identified and explored.*

The "What can I do with a major in ... ?" question can be answered directly.

7.. *The decision-making process is learned in a safe environment.* Helping students become aware of their own approaches to selecting a major can be dealt with in class.

The greatest advantage of a freshman orientation course or seminar is that students can experience personalized attention during the weeks that are identified as most conducive to attrition. Helping students negotiate the first months of college successfully facilitates their feeling more comfortable and self-confident about their new environment.

CAREER COURSES. Another group approach is the career-planning course for credit. Career courses can help students concentrate on the career-planning process and help them focus on specific areas of interest. Many career courses lead students through a series of decision-making steps. Gathering self-, academic and career information is an integral activity in most career courses. The small-group atmosphere also supports students while they are involved in this process.

Some career counselors create their own curriculum, but many others use courses that have been developed and researched by others. *Take Hold of Your Future: A Life/Career Planning Course,* published by the American College Testing Program (1982), and *Career Planning and Decision Making for College Students* by the Appalachia Education Laboratory (1979) are examples of courses that have been developed especially for college students.

Adviser Techniques

Effective advisers use many techniques and methods for helping undecided students. These include interviewing techniques that reflect proficient communication skills. Referral techniques are also important, since no one campus resource is adequate for providing undecided students with the wide breadth of information they need. Printed materials are another important advising tool. These techniques and skills need to become a part of all effective advising, regardless of the type of student being helped.

They are particularly important, however, in working with students who need to be guided and encouraged to negotiate the decision-making process in an expeditious way.

INTERVIEWING TECHNIQUES. Many undecided students have been helped to make a decision by discussing their situation over time with a caring adviser or counselor. Communication techniques such as reflecting and clarifying can be used to help students focus their thinking. Some suggestions for improving communication in the advising interview are:

1. *Opening* — Greet student by name. Be relaxed, warm. Open with a question, e.g. "How are things going?" or "How can I help?"

2. *Phrasing questions* — Conversational flow will be cut off if questions are asked so that a yes or no reply is all that is required. A good question might be, "What have you thought about taking next quarter?" or "What are some things that have made you think about business as a career?"

3. *Out-talking the student* — Good advising is effective listening, and listening is more than the absence of talking. Identify the fine shades of feelings behind the words.

4. *Accepting the student's attitudes and feelings* — Students may fear that advisers do not approve of what they say. Advisers must convey their acceptance of these feelings and attitudes in a nonjudgmental way. Cardinal principle: If the student thinks it is a problem, the adviser does, too.

5. *Cross-examining* — Do not fire questions at the student like a machine gun.

6. *Allowing silence in the interview* — Most people are embarrassed if no conversation is going on. Remember, the student may be groping for words or ideas.

7. *Reflecting the student's feelings* — Try to understand what the student is saying. For example, it is better to say, "You feel that your father expects you to major in premed" rather than, "Everyone has trouble getting along with his father sometimes."

8. *Admitting Your ignorance* — If a student asks a question regarding facts and you do not have them, admit it. Go to

your resources for the information immediately, or call the student back.

9. *Setting limits on the interview* — It is better if the adviser and the student realize from the beginning that the interview lasts for a fixed length of time.

10. *Ending the interview* — Once limits have been set, it is best to end the interview at the agreed time. A comfortable phrase might be, "Do you think we have done all we can for today?" or "Let's make another appointment so that we can go into this further."

The following probing questions are examples of what an adviser might use to help students articulate why they are undecided and help them become aware of certain aspects of the choice process they had not considered. Many undecided students simply need help in analyzing their needs before they can move forward in the exploration process. The questions are divided into three categories since information gathering sometimes falls into these three important areas.

Self-exploration

- As far back as you can remember, what general occupational fields have you thought of?
- What subjects did you enjoy in high school? In what subjects were your best grades?
- Do you consider your strengths to lie in the math/science areas or in the social sciences?
- What type of extracurricular activities did you take part in, in high school? What were the most enjoyable? What did you learn about yourself from them?
- What are your best personal qualities? What do your friends like most about you?
- What do you see as your limitations?
- Name the highest point in your life so far (your greatest accomplishment). What about the experience made it special?
- In what kind of work environment do you picture yourself, five years out of college?
- If you have a spare hour to use, what do you do?
- Why are you in college?

- What does a college degree mean to you?

Academic Major/Occupational Information

- What academic areas are you currently considering? What do you like about these areas?
- What occupations are you considering? What about these occupations attracts you?
- How do your abilities and skills fit the tasks necessary to succeed in these areas?
- Will these occupations provide the rewards and satisfactions you want for your life? Why?
- What are the differences between the two majors (occupations) you are tentatively considering? The similarities?
- Who has influenced your ideas about these alternatives?

Decision Making

- Do you ever have trouble making decisions? Little ones? Important ones?
- How do you generally go about making a decision? Describe the process.
- What specific strategies do you use?
- Do you use the same method for all types of decisions?
- Would you describe yourself as a spontaneous or a systematic decision-maker?
- Do you make decisions by yourself or do you need other people's opinions first?
- Are you feeling anxious about deciding on a major? Pressured? Why?
- How long do you think it will take you to make a decision? How long do you *want* it to take?

As discussed before, indecisive students with personal blocks to making a decision may require psychological counseling by a trained expert. Students with severe psychological problems often do not benefit from the types of interviewing or communication techniques outlined above. Advisers need to be sensitive in identifying these students and to make appropriate referrals as soon as the difficulty is discerned.

REFERRAL TECHNIQUES. Learning when and how to refer a

student to a selected resource is an important advising skill: Referring too quickly or too broadly can create a situation that adds to the student's confusion. Students should have an understanding of what areas of study they are considering before a referral is made. They need to have analyzed how their past academic record fits these areas, and and they need some knowledge of the major requirements involved. The referral resource can then refine the student's understanding of this particular area. Students often need help in formulating-questions before they make contact with the referral source, and advisers can help them frame questions that will ensure the most efficient use of the time.

Setting up an organized network of resources is another important aspect of referral. All resource persons on campus associated with academic information, for example, need to be aware of their responsibility to the referred student. Providing information in a clear and organized way can help students analyze and integrate it later. The network should include all academic and student service resources on campus. The adviser referring and the recipient of referrals need to work together so that the purpose and content of these contacts are clearly defined. A list of names, addresses, and phone numbers as well as areas of expertise should be widely disseminated among advisers, faculty, and student affairs personnel.

PRINTED MATERIALS. Advisers need to have in their possession comprehensive printed resources that can be used directly with the student. Curriculum sheets listing all requirements for a major, for example, can be useful in helping undecided students understand exactly what courses and sequences are required in a major. When these sheets are in the form of checklists, the student and adviser can monitor progress as well. These sheets should reflect immediately any change in curriculum, so that information is always current. Although college catalogs and bulletins typically contain information about academic programs, disposable curriculum sheets are conducive to making notes and recording personal information. Providing this structure helps take the mystery out of curricular information and clarifies all the requirements for a degree.

Other printed information can be created to serve the unique needs of the institution and the individual student on that campus.

The adviser's manual mentioned in Chapter 2, for example, is a critical printed resource for both adviser and student, and booklets containing the location and purpose of student services can provide important information for the student and adviser.

Adviser Training

Advisers working with undecided students have special needs. There are certain kinds and levels of expertise required to work effectively with students who are in the process of making educational and career decisions. The following outlines some of the elements that might be included as part of a new adviser training program or as in-service content for an established program. The background and experience of an adviser must be taken into consideration: Faculty advisers working with undecided students may need a greater emphasis on student and career development concerns, while full-time professional advisers may, on the other hand, need more training in academic information. There are certain content areas that all training programs need to emphasize, however (Ender and Winston, 1982; Gordon, 1980).

STUDENT DEVELOPMENT. As stated previously, many undecided students go through a normal transition period as they enter college and are in need of certain kinds of advising as these changes occur. Advisers working with undecided students need to be aware of student development theory and concepts so they are prepared to recognize and acknowledge individual differences among students. Advisers need to be aware of students' struggles to develop competencies, their need to establish interpersonal relationships, and their need to become autonomous (Chickering, 1969). Helping students identify, clarify, and prioritize their personal values and goals is an important task that take place within the advising relationship.

Training advisers in student development concepts enhances their perceptions of students as unique, developing individuals. This framework for advising undecided students answers many questions regarding the reasons for indecision and provides advising techniques that can reflect student needs.

CAREER DEVELOPMENT. Like student development theory, career development concepts help explain many of the so-called problems of undecided students. Many advisers from an academic background are not aware of this theory. A review of the theoretical frameworks of Holland (1973), Super (1957), and Tiedeman and O'Hara (1963), for example, can provide a working knowledge of how students explore, crystallize, and clarify decisions relating to career. Advisers with this background knowledge can begin to recognize different stages of the decision-making process as students begin to identify and explore alternatives. Advisers can then individualize their advising approach to suit each student's needs.

Advisers also need a working knowledge of how the student's interests, values, and abilities form a unique set of personal characteristics. They need to be able to recognize when a student may need referral for this type of self-assessment.

GENERAL ACADEMIC INFORMATION. Undecided students' interests and abilities cover such a wide range of programs that becoming a generalist adviser is absolutely essential. Advisers need to be able to discuss all the possible options that a student may present in an advising exchange. This means that their training must familiarize them with academic requirements that are both special and general. Possible career opportunities for each major must also be known, since it is often impossible for students to separate them. Being a generalist adviser does not require an in-depth knowledge of each major, but does it mean that one adviser must have ideas that cut across many different academic areas or degree programs.

When advisers are knowledgeable about exploratory courses in many disciplines, they can suggest courses that will help students experience different areas. Generalist advisers know enough about the academic offerings at their institutions to provide an initial introduction to any option the student may be considering. This knowledge may be too extensive or complex to assimilate during one training program. This implies that extended training is needed, and a series of workshops or in-service programs must be initiated to provide additional information.

Much of this information should be presented to the adviser in the form of an advisement manual. The training program can then provide more refined approaches. Perhaps no training topic is more important than academic program and requirement information. Methods for providing undecided students with this information in an organized way are also important.

REFERRAL AGENTS. Advisers need to be trained in how, when, and where to refer. Once students have identified options, advisers need to have an organized referral system in place. Introducing advisers to the other people in the academic information network helps to make the referral more personal and accurate.

Referrals may also be made to other campus resources such as study skills or tutoring centers, career-planning and placement offices, and counseling or health services. Training programs can familiarize advisers with all these resources by making actual site visits or by asking representatives of these services to explain their mission and function during the training program. Although it is often assumed that referral skills are automatically acquired, very often they need to be taught. Referring too quickly (before the student is ready) or broadly may be detrimental rather than helpful.

Other possible training content areas include campus policies and procedures, communication techniques, and course content and teaching skills, if the adviser is responsible for small-group advising or a freshman seminar section. After an extended period of time, advisers may have suggestions for topics for other in-service programs. Their expressed needs should be the basis for future training efforts. These needs may be assessed by listening to verbal suggestions or solicited through written questionnaires or checklists (Gordon, 1984; Hartman & Lagowski, 1982).

Program Evaluation

When evaluating a program, several factors must be considered. The first is *why* evaluation is needed. Greater accountability is often required during times of fiscal uncertainty or restrictions, for example: Being able to show positive outcomes of a program can often ensure its continuance. If the mission of higher education is to foster academic and personal growth of its students, then evaluation must become a critical function of any program. There are rarely perfect programs, so evaluation can help pinpoint where changes need to be made or which new program components have met their objectives. Understanding the effect of services on the personal and intellectual growth of undecided students is perhaps the major impetus toward establishing a comprehensive evaluation program.

The next consideration is *what* needs to be evaluated. This is why the objectives set for program and services (discussed in Chapter 2) are important. What needs to be evaluated depends on the desired outcomes already established. For example, is one of the program's objectives that undecided students acquire knowledge? If so, what kind of knowledge? Occupational knowledge? Academic knowledge? Self-knowledge?

Does the program attempt to change student attitudes toward work? Toward certain academic possibilities? Toward themselves? Does it attempt to change students' behavior? How does it foster information-seeking behavior, if this is a goal of the program? Does it attempt to make students aware of their personal growth over a period of time? The adviser may observe this change, but does the student? If a student makes a decision as a result of the program, is that decision stable over time? There are many variables that can be measured within an evaluation system based on set objectives.

Some campuses are concerned about student attrition, and, since undecided students are considered a high-risk group in this regard, evaluation can include projections of or actual figures on the retention of undecided students. Questioning students as they withdraw is a valuable source of information about the effectiveness and accessibility of services for students, for example.

What is evaluated comes from the well–thought-out objectives of the total program and also its parts. Both the students' and the advisers' perceptions of how well these objectives are being met are included.

The last consideration of an evaluation program is *how* to evaluate. The methods used depend on what is being measured. A standardized instrument or a simple, locally developed questionnaire can help determine the progress students are making in identifying and implementing academic and career choices. The *Career Decision Scale* (Osipow, 1980) mentioned earlier may be used as a pre- and postintervention evaluation to show how individuals or groups of undecided students have changed as a result of a specific intervention. Simple questionnaires have been developed to measure the level of indecision about a major and career among students (Goodson, 1981; Harren, 1978; Kimes & Troth, 1974).

Behavioral changes may be measured by simple checklists or through standardized instruments. Crites' *Career Maturity Inventory* (CMI) (1973) measures attitudes and knowledge about work and can provide important data for program effectiveness as well as for individual student counseling.

As to *when* to evaluate, there are many points at which evaluation may be accomplished. When undecided students finally declare a major, that is an excellent time to ask simple questions about their reactions to and satisfaction with the help they have received. Alternatively, each program element, such as workshops or classes, may be formatively evaluated as it is completed. Interviewing random samples of undecided students also may provide insights into how students perceive, participate in, and react to specific program elements.

Evaluating a total program is also important. Summative evaluations may be performed at the end of each school term or at the end of a year. While there are commercial products available to conduct an evaluation, it is sometimes more efficient to create one that reflects local program objectives. In any case, data describing the effectiveness of a program are imperative for administrators making budget decisions.

Evaluating advisers' contributions to the program is also important. There are several approaches to overall adviser evaluation. Evaluation of an adviser's performance from students' perspectives may be accomplished by a simple questionnaire during the scheduling period, for example. If adviser evaluation procedures are already in place, a few additional questions on the form, regarding undecided students, may provide more detailed information about the special services created for them. Advisers may also be asked to evaluate their own performance, including their reactions to the materials provided them, their suggestions for administrative changes, or the need for new or different program directions. Advisers' immediate supervisors may also evaluate their performance. Many advisers appreciate positive suggestions for improving their skills. They also need to hear praise when they have performed a task well.

As with any evaluation effort, one person must be responsible for coordinating the whole. One individual needs to be responsible for gathering the information, analyzing it, and disseminating it to the persons involved. If changes are to be made, they must be based on current, accurate information from both students' and advisers' perspectives. In this way a program will continue to reflect the ongoing, changing needs of the students for whom it exists.

RESEARCH. Evaluation efforts often provide information that would be helpful to other campuses involved in the same or similar programs. Many campuses have gathered data about their undecided students but do not consider it important enough to write up for broader dissemination. If data is carefully gathered and statistically evaluated, evaluation results may be written up for submission to professional journals. This is why well-formed objectives and outcome statements are critical. New programs can more realistically shape their efforts when established programs share experiences that have been successful and carefully evaluated.

Summary

Many program elements may be created to help undecided students make educational and career decisions. Individual students may be served through testing programs, which can foster knowledge about interests, abilities, values, and other personal characteristics. Career libraries and computerized career information systems can also provide resources for self-assessment, as well as academic and occupational information. Programmed modules containing self-assessment activities leading into an occupational classification system can also be used in advising an individual student.

Group advising can take place through workshops on many topics, such as decision making, goal setting, exploring academic alternatives, and relating personality measures to careers. Freshman orientation seminars and career-planning courses for credit provide a structured format in which undecided students can explore within a given time frame.

Adviser techniques and methods are important aspects of a successful program. Advisers need to be proficient in communication skills, so that they can relate to students in a personal way. Advisers need good referral techniques to help students make informative and productive contacts. Printed materials are also critical to good advising. Making sure materials are current and accurate is an adviser's responsibility.

When training advisers who work with undecided students, certain topics are especially relevant. Knowledge of student and career development and academic information can be provided in a training program. Teaching advisers when, how, and where to refer students is also important.

Evaluation of a program for undecided students must be geared to the objectives that are initially set. Both formative and summative evaluation methods may be used, to ensure that both the individual components and the overall program are responsive to student needs. The overall program may be measured against the philosophy and mission statements that were established at the outset. Evaluation efforts must always reflect the unique needs and approaches that individual campuses use to serve their undecided student population.

REFERENCES

Appalachia Educational Laboratory. *Career Information System*. Bloomington, Illinois: McKnight, 1978.

Appalachia Educational Laboratory. *Career Planning and Decision Making for College Students*. Bloomington, Illinois: McKnight, 1979.

American College Testing Program. *Take Hold of Your Future: A Life/Career Planning Course*. Iowa City: American College Testing Program, 1982.

American College Testing Program. *VIESA*. Iowa City: American College Testing Program, 1983.

Buros, O. K. *Tests in Print*. Highland Park, N.J.: Gryphon Press, 1972.

Buros, O. K. (Ed.). *The Eighth Mental Measurement Yearbook* (2 vols.). Highland Park, N.J.: Gryphon Press, 1978.

Campbell, D. P. *Manual for the Strong-Campbell Interest Inventory*. Stanford, California: Stanford University Press, 1974.

Chickering, A. W. *Education and Identity*. San Francisco: Jossey-Bass, 1969.

Crites, J. O. *Theory and Career Research Handbook for the Career Maturity Inventory*. Monterey, California: CTB/McGraw-Hill, 1973.

Ender, S. C., and Winston, R. B. Training allied professional advisors. In R. B. Winston, S. C. Ender, and T. K. Miller (Eds.), *Developmental Approaches to Academic Advising*. San Francisco: Jossey-Bass, 1982.

Fitts, C. T., and Swift, F. H. *The Construction of Orientation Courses for College Freshmen*. University of California publications, vol. 2, No. 3, pp. 45–250. Berkeley: University of California Press, 1928.

Fuqua, D., and Hartman, B. A behavioral index of career indecision for college students. *Journal of College Student Personnel*, 1983, *24*, 507–512.

Goodson, W. Do career development needs exist for all students entering college or just the undecided major students? *Journal of College Student Personnel*, 1981, *22*, 413–417.

Goodstein, L. Behavior theoretical view of counseling. In B. Steffre (Ed.), *Theories of Counseling*. New York: McGraw-Hill, 1965, pp. 140–192.

Gordon, V., and Sears, S. J. *A Search for Common Elements Among Learning and Career Decision Making Styles*. Paper presented at the National Dissemination Conference for Educational Training for Human Development, Memphis, Tennessee, June, 1983.

Gordon, V. N. Training academic advisors: Content and method. *Journal of College Student Personnel*, 1980, *21*, 334–340.

———. Training professional and paraprofessional advisors. In R. Winston, T. Miller, S. Ender, and T. Grites (Eds.), *Academic Advising and Student Development*. San Francisco: Jossey-Bass, 1984.

Gottfredson, G., Holland, J., and Ogawa, D. *Dictionary of Holland Occupational Codes*. Palo Alto, California: Consulting Psychologists Press, 1982.

Harren, V. *Assessment of Career Decision Making*. Carbondale, Illinois: Southern Illinois University.

Hartman, B. W., and Fuqua, D. R. Career indecision from a multidimensional perspective: A reply to Grites. *School Counselor*, 1983, *30*, 340–346.

Hartman, N., and Lagowski, J. Performance evaluation of peer advisors. *Journal of College Student Personnel*, 1982, *23*, 78–79.

Holland, J. L. *Making Vocational Choices: A Theory of Careers*. Englewood Cliffs, N.J.: Prentice-Hall, 1973.

———. *Self-Directed Search*. Palo Alto, California: Consulting Psychologists Press, 1977.

Kimes, H., and Troth, W. Relationship of trait anxiety to career decisiveness. *Journal of Counseling Psychology*, 1974, *21*, 277–280.

Kuder, G. F. A rationale for evaluating interests. *Educational and Psychological Measurement*, 1963, *23*, 3–10.

Myers, I. B. *Gifts Differing*. Palo Alto, California: Consulting Psychologists Press, 1980.

Osipow, S. H. *Manual for the Career Decision Scale*. Columbus, Ohio: Marathon Consulting and Press, 1980.

Osipow, S. H. *Theories of Career Development* (3rd ed.). Englewood Cliffs, N.J.: Prentice-Hall, 1983.

Pinkney, J. W. The *Myers-Briggs Type Indicator* as an alternative in career counseling. *Personnel and Guidance Journal*, 1983, *62*, 173–177.

Rees, P., and Fischer, C. *Interactive Computer Advisement: Development of a Model.* Paper presented at the Seventh National Conference on Academic Advising, St. Louis, Missouri, October, 1983.

Simon, S. B., Howe, L. W., and Kirschenbaum, H. *A Handbook of Practical Strategies for Teachers and Students.* New York: Hart, 1972.

Super, D. E. *The Psychology of Careers.* New York: Harper & Row, 1957.

Tiedeman, D., and O'Hara, R. *Career Development: Choice and Adjustment.* New York: College Entrance Examination Board, 1963.

Zunker, V. G. *Using Assessment Results in Career Counseling.* Monterey, California: Brooks/Cole, 1982.

Chapter 6

MODEL PROGRAMS
FOR UNDECIDED STUDENTS

When initiating or refining a program for undecided students, it is often helpful to know what organizational structures other institutions have used and how certain programmatic components or activities have been implemented. Each campus is unique, and the final form of any program reflects the academic and career advising structures and delivery systems that are already in place. For example, what type of general advising system does the institution have? Is there a career center? Is there a career library or computerized system already in place? A program for undecided students must be integrated into many existing resources.

Habley (1983) discusses different advising model systems and describes how an institution's organizational structure influences the type of advising program a campus develops. Effective programs have assessed student needs, have established efficient communication and information flow patterns, and have in place a system for coordination and supervision. The delivery system used to provide services for undecided students depends on the organizational structure in which the program resides.

The American College Testing Program conducted a national survey of over 700 institutions to identify the types and scope of services being provided for undecided students across the country (Crockett, Silberhorn & Kaufman, 1981). Some of the program elements and institutional approaches described below are reported in that study.

Identifying Undecided Students

According to the ACT survey, a majority of institutions identify undecided students through admissions data. Others institutions identify these students through an advising or registrar's office. Orientation is used by some to determine the undecided group, while others rely on information provided by college entrance examinations.

The names used by institutions to describe this population vary as well. Almost half use the term *undecided*, while many others use *undeclared. General education, general studies, exploratory, liberal arts,* and *open-major* are terms used by a smaller number of institutions to describe students who are uncommitted to a direction as they begin college.

Delivery Systems

The methods for assigning advisers to undecided students vary among the institutions surveyed by the American College Testing Program. A majority are assigned to specially designated faculty advisers or counselors. A very small number of programs make random assignments to faculty advisers. A large number of two– and four-year public institutions assign undecided students to special nonfaculty advisers/counselors.

When asked at what point students are required to declare a major, the largest group indicates by the end of the sophomore year. Two-year institutions compose the largest group indicating that a declaration of major is not required. Others require a declaration of major at varying times during the freshman year.

The primary mode for delivering advising services to undecided students, as reported by the ACT survey, is individual contacts or a combination of individual and group contacts. Very few use a group or class approach exclusively.

Large universities such as Ohio State University (Gordon, 1981), Michigan State University (Kishler, 1981), Indiana University-Purdue University (IUPU) (Merkler, 1981) and Bowling Green State University (Morgan, 1981) use a university college or division structure to advise undecided students. Undecided students thus are part of an initial enrollment unit that has special responsibility for advising freshmen and sophomores. This type of college or division, as described in Chapter 2, can serve undecided students within a general advising unit and can offer the specialized advising and program components that undecided students require.

Ohio State University encourages students with many ideas or no ideas for a major to spend a year on organized exploration and information gathering (Gordon, 1979). Students are assigned to an adviser who is a generalist in academic information and trained as a career adviser as well. This combination helps integrate the academic/career problem that many undecided students have trouble resolving. Many of these advisers are graduate students who are in educational counseling, student personnel, counseling psychology, or related programs. Many have had experiences in career development theory and practice prior to being selected for this task.

The undergraduate university division at Michigan State University is administratively responsible for freshman and sophomore students. No-preference students are housed within the university division. Michigan State's program for no-preference majors is staffed by an associate director and part-time professional advisers. Since the expertise needed to advise no-preference students takes so long to develop, Michigan State prefers to train part-time professionals who will be more stable in their employment over time. Another important feature of Michigan State's program is the establishment of three residence hall satellite offices. Students have access to the same professional advising in four locations.

Advising of open option students at Iowa State University provides academic and career advising services to students within a College of Sciences and Humanities (Beatty, Davis & White, 1983). This delivery model provides two types of adviser involvement: (1) full-time professional advisers in the dean's office, and (2) faculty advisers within the dean's office. Faculty advisers are assigned students who are interested in broad areas, such as sciences, arts, and social sciences. These faculty hold half-time advising appointments in the Open Options Advising Center. This system was devised after a study was conducted by the College of Sciences and Humanities to determine students' assessment of the effectiveness of their advisers. The present system was established to integrate faculty advising into the total program for advising undecided students.

The Academic Exploration Program (AEP) at Bradley University is an example of a faculty advising system with strong coordination provided by the Office of Student Planning (Huddleston & Goldenburg, 1981). Since the undecided student needs accessibility to many academic departments and student services, Bradley's approach integrates the resources of academic and student affairs in an effective way.

The University of Northern Iowa established an Academic Advising Services Center to advise first-year students and other undergraduates who need help in selecting and planning their academic programs (Abel, 1981a; 1981b). Advising is provided by two full-time professional advisers, residence hall coordinators, and ten peer advisers. Faculty advisers are assigned to freshmen who have indicated a major preference. Undecided students are assigned to either the professional staff in the Center or to residence hall coordinators. Training residence hall coordinators to fill this role is viewed as an effective way to bridge academic and student services. This approach stresses the importance of advisers becoming involved in the students' entire college experience.

Missouri Western State College uses a system of faculty advising for undecided students coordinated by the director of counseling and testing (McDonald, 1981). Faculty advise in the Counseling and Testing Office during a two-week preadvisement period, since it was found that students came to that location in greater numbers than they did to individual faculty offices.

George Mason University exemplifies an Advising Center system created especially for undeclared majors (Looney, 1981). The director of the Center reports to the associate vice-president for academic affairs. The Center is staffed by a full-time director, who also has administrative responsibility for orientation. Five part-time advisers complete the staff. The Center also works with students who are in the process of changing their major.

Eastern Kentucky University's Undeclared Student Program is a part of the Office of Undergraduate Studies (Schwendeman, 1981). Many areas are included in the Office of Undergraduate Studies: advising and student records, learning skills, and counseling and career development services. The program for undecided students is incorporated within the overall academic support services provided by this office. Students are assigned to specially selected advisers and are provided career counseling and information by other units within the Office of Undergraduate Studies.

Two-year institutions are discovering a need to develop special services for undecided students. Elizabethtown Community College in Kentucky has created an advising center specifically for undeclared majors (Thomas, 1981). Specially designated faculty advisers are assigned to work with this clientele. The general studies area is assigned responsibility for advising undecided students at North Shore Community College in Massachusetts (German, 1981). The specially assigned faculty advisers are from the student's major career interest area. Many two-year institutions offer services to undecided students through their counseling centers or career counselors when no administrative link is established.

These programs are examples of the variety of administrative approaches used to provide special attention to undecided students on campuses of all sizes, types, and organizational structures. Almost all report that their programs have positive effects on student satisfaction and retention.

Program Components

Many program elements are described by the institutions in the ACT study. One-to-one advising is stressed by almost all those surveyed. Michigan State, Ohio State, and Bowling Green State University stress the importance of well-trained staff, so that the individual advising function can be as effective as possible. Faculty advisers at Missouri Western State College are asked to assimilate eight major points of information in their ongoing contacts with students:

1. Academic abilities (high school record, grade point average, ACT scores)
2. High school background (courses taken)
3. Work hours versus college hours (two hours' study for one semester hour needed)
4. Family obligations and other demands on time

5. Interests of the student
6. Motivation of the student
7. Orientation of the student to college
8. Past performance/high school rank/study habits

Missouri Western State emphasizes communication skills as a critical tool for advising undecided students.

Preregistration is an important part of Michigan State's program, as well as those of other institutions. It is felt that undecided students need more in-depth advising at this particular time than declared majors. Course exploration as a vehicle for exposing students to a variety of academic disciplines is stressed in the Ohio State and IUPU programs. Many departments offer these introductory courses to help students learn about their particular discipline.

The State University College of Arts and Sciences at Plattsburg, New York, offers a miniworkshop for undecided students during its freshman orientation program (Corigliano & Morocco, 1979). A decision-making model is introduced, with the discussion centering around the idea that not being declared at that point is a practical choice. Majors are introduced via an interest inventory. The program is rated as excellent by most students.

Topical workshops and minicourses for no credit are a feature of many programs for undecided students. The Advising Center at George Mason University offers a "Choosing/Changing Majors" workshop in cooperation with the Counseling Center. After the workshop experience, which teaches values clarification and decision-making skills, students are referred back to the Advising Center to explore some of the academic alternatives they have identified. The Exploratory Student Program (ESP) at IUPU provides minicourses and informational workshops that help students explore a variety of majors and career alternatives. "Educational Planning" workshops and a first-semester workshop for peer advisers are provided within the IUPU program.

Bradley offers a "Life Planning" seminar for no credit, while Ohio State University, Northern Missouri State (Cooper, 1981), the University of Northern Iowa, Georgia College (Sallstrom, 1981), and Eastern Kentucky offer orientation and/or career courses for credit.

The freshman seminar course for undecided students at the University of Maine integrates the values of the liberal arts with career exploration (McKerrow, Viletti & Gershman, 1979). Rather than offering a narrowly focused perspective on career exploration, the course concentrates on the values of training individuals who can remain flexible in a changing job market. The course is rated as an effective component of the program, since it involves all or most undecided students in an organized vehicle for exploration.

Testing is offered by all programs in either an advisement, a career-planning and placement, or a counseling center. IUPU uses an interest inventory to begin an organized exploring of both majors and careers. A special guide to majors has been developed by the Exploratory Students Program staff. Bradley has also developed a well-known students' guide for exploring majors and relating them to career possibilities.

Career libraries are considered an important component of many programs, especially those of Lewis University (Stojan, 1981), Bradley University, and Ohio State University. Library facilities are organized to provide career information in an easily accessible way. The *Career Information System*, mentioned in Chapter 5, has been implemented as an organizational system by several programs. Computerized career information systems are listed by Northwestern Missouri and Eastern Kentucky as integral to their advising undecided students.

Community programs are mentioned by several institutions. The Partners in Education Program at Ohio State University contains the names of 1000 alumni who have volunteered to discuss their careers with students. The Footsteps Program at Bradley University is a one-day cooperative educational experience. Students may make as many contacts as they wish in both programs.

The Advising Center at George Mason University publishes a monthly newsletter that provides information about academic programs, publicizes programs and services offered on campus, and includes additional information useful to both undecided students and staff.

At Elizabethtown Community College, career guidance sessions and testing are offered to undecided students. A special follow-up mailing is sent to undecided students at the end of each semester.

Both an orientation course and a career/life-planning course for credit are offered by North Shore Community College. Workshops on decision making and academic skill building are also provided.

Many of the model programs report a wide variety of activities and services for undecided students, including those originating in the unit responsible for this group and those offered by other campus offices. The effective integration of these services seems to be an important part of a successful program.

Adviser Selection and Training

Faculty and full-time professional advisers working with undecided students are carefully selected on most campuses in the survey. Very few advisers are selected randomly. This indicates the importance attached to the special knowledge and skills that advisers need in working with this group. Ongoing in-service training is another important component of a successful program. Ohio State and Michigan State Universities emphasize the need for intensive and individualized training in order to develop and maintain the competence that such a demanding task requires. All programs emphasized that the adviser selection and training process is an important aspect of their overall effort.

Summary

Many model programs for undecided students are evolving in all types of institutions across the country. Many of these successful programs incorporate similar activities and services. All emphasize the need for individual student contact with carefully selected and trained advisers or counselors. Recognizing that small-group offerings are a benefit to many students, workshops and no-credit and credit courses in academic exploration and career planning are also included in most comprehensive programs.

All programs stress the necessity for establishing a coordinating effort, since the needs of undecided students cut across many campus offices and resources. Each program reflects the unique organizational structure of the institution and the importance attached to serving the needs of this special groups of college students.

REFERENCES

Abel, J. A center for undecided students. In D. Crockett, C. Silberhorn, and J. Kaufman (Eds.), *Campus Practices for Students with Undeclared Majors.* Iowa City: American College Testing Program, 1981a.

Abel, J. Residence hall coordinators: Academic advising for "undecided students." *NACADA Journal,* 1981b, *1,* 44–46.

Beatty, J., Davis, B., and White, B. Open option advising at iowa state university: An integrated advising and career planning model. *NACADA Journal,* 1983, *3,* 39–48.

Cooper, M. Students with undeclared majors. In D. Crockett, C. Silberhorn, and J. Kaufman (Eds.), *Campus Practices for Students with Undeclared Majors.* Iowa City: American College Testing Program, 1981.

Corigliano, T., and Morocco, P. Advising the undeclared student: Using a mini-workshop during freshman orientation. In D. Crockett (Ed.), *Academic Advising: A Resource Document.* Iowa City: American College Testing Program, 1979.

Crockett, D., Silberhorn, C., and Kaufman, J. (Eds.). *Campus Practices for Students with Undeclared Majors.* Iowa City: American College Testing Program, 1981.

German, K. L. *Response to "Survey of Campus Practices."* Iowa City: American College Testing Program, 1981.

Gordon, V. N. Integrating the academic and career advising process for exploratory students. In D. Crockett (Ed.), *Academic Advising: A Resource Document.* Iowa City: American College Testing Program, 1979.

——. Program for undecided students. In D. Crockett, C. Silberhorn, and J. Kaufman (Eds.), *Campus Practices for Students with Undeclared Majors.* Iowa City: American College Testing Program, 1981.

Habley, W. R. Organizational structure for academic advising: Models and implications. *Journal of College Student Personnel,* 1983, *24,* 535–540.

Huddleston, T. H., and Goldenburg, D. H. The student planning structure and the academic exploration program. In D. Crockett, C. Silberhorn, and J. Kaufman (Eds.), *Campus Practices for Students with Undeclared Majors.* Iowa City: American College Testing Program, 1981.

Kishler, T. C. No preference at Michigan State University. In D. Crockett, C. Silberhorn, and J. Kaufman (Eds.), *Campus Practices for Students with Undeclared Majors.* Iowa City: American College Testing Program, 1981.

Looney, S. Students with undeclared majors. In D. Crockett, C. Silberhorn, and J. Kaufman (Eds.), *Campus Practices for Students with Undeclared Majors.* Iowa City: American College Testing Program, 1981.

McDonald, M. Advisement system of undeclared majors. In D. Crockett, C. Silberhorn, and J. Kaufman (Eds.), *Campus Practices for Students with Undeclared Majors.* Iowa City: American College Testing Program, 1981.

McKerrow, R., Viletti, M., and Gershman, E. A model program for advising the undeclared major. In D. Crockett (Ed.), *Academic Advising: A Resource Document*. Iowa City: American College Testing Program, 1979.

Merkler, N. Campus practices for students with undeclared majors. In D. Crockett, C. Silberhorn, and J. Kaufman (Eds.), *Campus Practices for Students with Undeclared Majors*. Iowa City: American College Testing Program, 1981.

Morgan, J. University division center for educational options. In D. Crockett, C. Silberhorn, and J. Kaufman (Eds.), *Campus Practices for Students with Undeclared Majors*. Iowa City: American College Testing Program, 1981.

Sallstrom, J. E. Students with undecided majors. In D. Crockett, C. Silberhorn, and J. Kaufman (Eds.), *Campus Practices for Students with Undeclared Majors*. Iowa City: American College Testing Program, 1981.

Schwendeman, J. Program for undeclared majors. In D. Crockett, C. Silberhorn, and J. Kaufman (Eds.), *Campus Practices for Students with Undeclared Majors*. Iowa City: American College Testing Program, 1981.

Stojan, S. Students with undeclared majors. In D. Crockett, C. Silberhorn, and J. Kaufman (Eds.), *Campus Practices for Students with Undeclared Majors*. Iowa City: American College Testing Program, 1981.

Thomas, R. B. *Response to "Survey of Campus Practices"*. Iowa City: American College Testing Program, 1981.

AUTHOR INDEX

SUBJECT INDEX

Deliberate psychological education, 15
Delivery systems, 109–115
Department of Labor, 81, 87, 89
Developmental advising, 16, 17, 55,
    65–85
Developmental skill deficits, 43
Developmental stages and tasks, 17, 66, 67,
    68, 83
Diagnosis, 7, 77–78
Differential Aptitude Tests, 87
DISCOVER, 81, 91
Dogmatism, 9
Dualistic students, 66, 68

E

Eastern Kentucky University, 111, 113,
    114
Economic factors, 17
Elizabethtown Community College, 112,
    114
Employment skills, 12
Energy level, 45
Engineering students, 54
Entering freshmen, 42–46, 61
Evaluation, 35, 101–104, 105

F

Faculty advising, 26, 27–28, 33, 39,
    94, 109
Family background, 9
Follow-up, 83

G

General Aptitude Test Battery, 87
George Mason University, 111, 113
Georgia College, 113
Goals, 12, 16, 45, 51, 59, 74, 114
Graduates, undecided, 10
Group advising/counseling, 13, 35, 46, 58,
    92–93, 104

H

High school background, 9
Holland personality types, 81, 89
Honors students, 56–57, 61
Humanitarian orientation, 5

I

Identifying undecided students, 108
Identity, 5, 10·
Indecision, vii, 5, 8
    antecedents, 3–7, 17, 45, 75–77
    choice patterns, 4
    levels, 9, 71, 78
Indecisiveness, 4, 14, 45
Indiana University-Purdue University,
    109, 113, 114
Individual counseling, 15, 16, 86–92,
    115
Information gathering, 5, 15, 80–81
Informational deficits, 43
Integrating academic and career services,
    38
Intellectual curiosity, 8
Interests, 5, 8, 9, 45, 56, 76, 87
Interventions, 11–16, 17, 43
Interviewing techniques, 95
Iowa State University, 110

J

Jackson Vocational Interest Survey, 87

K

Kuder Vocational Preference Record,
    87

L

Lewis University, 114
Library, career, 35, 86, 89–90, 104
Life goals, 9

M

Major-changers, vii, viii, 46–54,
    61
Maturity, 10, 14, 66, 72–74, 83
Michigan State University, 109, 110, 112,
    115
Missouri Western State College, 111, 112,
    113
Moral development, 15
Motivation, 11, 47, 48
Multiplicity, 76